W9-APL-783

"There is no such thing as a perfect parent; we learn to become the best parent we can be."

Stephen Gross

THE SIMPLEST BABY BOOK IN THE WORLD

Copyright © 2021 Simplest Company LLC.

All rights reserved.

All the text and artwork in this book are copyright ©2021 Simplest Company.
This book or any portion thereof may not be reproduced, stored in a retrieval system, or transmitted, in any form or by any means, electronic, mechanical, photocopying, recording or distributing any part of it in any form without prior written permission from the publisher.

Printed in China
First Edition, October 2021

Paperback ISBN: 9781736894705

Library of Congress Control Number: 2021907399

To order additional copies of this book or for volume purchases and resale

inquiries to: info@simplestbaby.com
Published by Simplest Company
Los Angeles, CA
simplestbaby.com

Illustrations by Stephen Gross

Copyright © 2021 Simplest Company LLC.
Simplest Baby is the registered trademark of Simplest Company LLC.

Note: All babies are unique, and this book is not intended to substitute for the advice of your pediatrician or other physician who should be consulted on all infant matters, especially if the baby is showing any signs of illness or out-of-the-ordinary behavior.

THE SIMPLEST BABY

BOOK IN THE WORLD

**You Got This!
The Illustrated, Grab-and-Do
Guide for a Healthy, Happy Baby**

Stephen Gross

Jeremy F. Shapiro, MD, MPH, FAAP

Gabriella Terhes Karlsson, Newborn Care Specialist/Doula/
Sleep Trainer

and the Simplest Baby Community

DEDICATION

Becoming a father has taught me a lot, and it is difficult to express just how much. It has given me a whole new understanding and appreciation of the effort that parents go through.

To my sister, let me say, **WOW, RESPECT, RESPECT, RESPECT!** My sister was a stay-at-home mom who got divorced after seven years of marriage. She then had to get back into the job market and raised two boys on her own. OMG, I can't imagine working and taking care of the kids alone. After all this, her boys have grown up to be amazing young men—well-adjusted, well-mannered, and successful. She obviously did a lot of things right, and it must have been extraordinarily difficult. To you, I say, I'm sorry—sorry for not understanding all of this at the time (Typical Guy) and for not being a more supportive brother.

You may not realize it, but you have been an inspiration to me and one of the reasons I wrote this book. When they say it takes a village to raise children, it's true. But, not all of us are close to our family or have others who can help us. My hope is that this book will help other moms, dads, and caregivers who, like you, have to basically do it all—and that **Simplest Baby** might become a part of other new parents' extended village. May it lend a little help like so many have done for me and you.

I love you dearly, and thank you for being my big sister.

Steve

MY STORY

As a new dad, I didn't know much about raising kids and didn't have a strong support group, living far from our families. I found the information out there—books, websites, blogs, videos, etc.—all too dense, overwhelming, and not simple enough for today's needs.

I did a lot of research through countless conversations with a community of those who know best—moms, dads, nurses, doctors, nannies, etc.—and distilled it to the essentials.

I realized that if I had this challenge, other new parents must too.

And that is where the idea for Simplest Baby came from: to share this collective knowledge in a way that provides new parents with the solutions they need quickly and easily, and to create a safe place that invites parents to share and support each other.

WHY YOU NEED THIS BOOK

For this book, I assume you:

- Are pregnant or have a baby under one year of age.

- Are interested in learning how to take good care of your child.

- Don't have time to go through 600+ page books.

- Are tired of getting random information from friends, family, and the internet.

- Want your baby to sleep through the night.

- Want simple, predictable feeding, napping, and play habits.

- Want your baby to be healthy, happy, safe, and well-adjusted.

- Want to buy what your baby really needs and not overspend.

- Want recommendations about the best products.

- Want to take back control of your life.

- Want to spend more time enjoying the journey of parenthood.

SIMPLEST BABY
HOW IT WORKS

1. **START BY UNDERSTANDING THE BIG PICTURE**

Clear development phases outlined so you understand the time frames for your baby to achieve certain goals.

2. **GET ON THE SIMPLEST BABY PLAN**™

Following Simplest Baby's schedules will help you get things under control and help baby achieve key milestones.

AND SAVE BY BUYING ONLY

Each section outlines the things you will need and not more.

Shop & Blog

Go to **Simplestbaby.com** for specific recommendations on the smartest baby products, must-have essentials, and informative posts.

TIPS & SHORTCUTS

Sprinkled throughout the book you will find these helpful tips

 QUICK TIP — Small practical recommendations that help make life just a little easier.

 Daddy Hack — Dad's simple solutions and clever work-arounds for everyday baby issues.

 3. **APPLY OUR SIMPLEST DIRECTIONS**

Learn about the key functions, essential practices, and topics that are most pressing.

 Eat

  Sleep

 Poop

 Bath

 Play

PLUS

LEARN THE BASICS YOU NEED TO KNOW

Topics include:

 Care

 Clothing

 Safety

 Travel

  Health

 Support

 Staying Sane

THE MUST-HAVE STUFF!

Simplest Baby Community

Join the community to find answers to your questions, share your experiences, or just get a little encouragement.

CONTENTS

PLAY & LEARN

The essential things to know about baby exercises, socialization, sharing, screen time, childcare, and more.

PAGES: 125–138

BABY CARE

Personal care essentials for baby and everything you will need.

PAGES: 139–154

CLOTHING

The essential list of clothing for your baby as she grows.

PAGES: 155–164

SAFETY

Tips on keeping your baby safe, including babyproofing, avoiding choking hazards, and managing pets.

PAGES: 165–188

OUT & ABOUT

What you need to know about going mobile with baby, with tips on going to restaurants, traveling by car, plane, and more.

PAGES: 189–214

HEALTH

The most common health-related issues you might experience and what to do about them.

PAGES: 215–250

SUPPORT

Learn about the basic types of support from childcare, nannies, babysitters, and more.

PAGES: 251–260

STAYING SANE

Starting a new family can be tremendously stressful. This section gives tips on taking care of yourself and dealing with stress.

PAGES: 261–274

Sometimes
the smallest things
take up the most
room in your heart.

PREPARING FOR BABY

What you really need to know and prepare before the big day arrives

THE MUST-HAVES

FOR THE NURSERY

1 CRIB

The crib should be sturdy and have fixed sides with the space between slats no larger than $2^{3/8}$ inches apart. Look for one made of eco-friendly, sustainable materials that use nontoxic paint. The headboard should be solid with no decorative cutouts or post embellishments that a child's clothing could get caught on.

1 MATTRESS

Look for a firm mattress about six inches deep. It should be hypoallergenic and free of phthalates, lead, and mercury. It should fit snugly in the crib with no space between the mattress and the crib sides. Greenguard certified.

2 WATERPROOF MATTRESS COVERS

Look for a fitted, waterproof cover that is breathable and hypoallergenic.

2 to 3 FITTED CRIB SHEETS

100 percent organic fitted crib sheets made of fabrics that are either woven cottons, cotton blends, or lightweight flannel.

1 SMOKE DETECTOR

A smoke detector should be inside every sleeping room in your home, including the nursery.

1 CHAIR

Look for a sturdy, comfortable rocker or glider with wide, padded armrests and good back support. Make sure there are no exposed moving parts or gaps in the structure that could trap or pinch fingers. The ability to swivel and recline are pluses.

1 CARBON MONOXIDE DETECTOR

This device detects carbon monoxide (CO) gas in order to prevent poisoning.

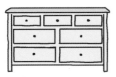

1 DRESSER

We suggest a sturdy dresser with several drawers. We recommend a long, low dresser so you can secure a changing pad to the top of it and avoid purchasing a separate changing table.

1 BABY MONITOR

Choose a video or wireless monitor that can be recharged or plugged in. Night vision provides a clearer image when the lights are low or off. It should have the ability to zoom in and turn so when the baby moves, it can follow. One with the ability to monitor the room temperature is a plus.

1 LAUNDRY HAMPER

You will need a laundry hamper for all the many dirty clothes, bibs, sheets, burp cloths, etc.

1 DIAPER PAIL

Choose a tall waterproof pail with good capacity that has a filter or some other device for odor control. Look for a pail with a foot pedal to open.

1 MESH CRIB LINER

Not a must, but it can be very helpful to prevent baby's arms and legs from getting stuck between crib slats. It's made of a lightweight, breathe-through mesh, with no padding to restrict airflow. This is not a bumper—bumpers should never be used in a crib due to the risk of SIDS.

GET THE RIGHT STUFF!
Go to Simplestbaby.com for recommendations of the smartest baby products and essentials.

REDUCE VOCs

As you purchase all the fun items you'll need for the nursery, you should be aware that many of these beautiful new items may expose your baby to some potentially harmful chemicals: VOCs.

WHAT ARE VOCs: VOLATILE ORGANIC COMPOUNDS?

They are gases that many household items give off under normal indoor conditions, affecting the quality of the air in the home.

These chemicals are part of the manufacturing process and can be found in mattresses, carpets, paints, clothing, and even toys. They create fumes that can make you and your baby sick. Over time these chemicals do dissipate, but it takes a while.

TIPS TO REDUCE THE RISK OF VOCs

Start Early

Start preparing the nursery early so that you can let the room air out for a month before your little bundle of joy arrives.

Painting

When painting the nursery, choose ultra-low-VOC, zero-VOC, or water-based paints. You will still want to leave time for ample ventilation.

Flooring

Flooring can have lots of VOCs depending on what you use, especially carpet. Carpeting made from natural, VOC-free materials such as wool, cotton, sisal, or jute are all better choices than carpets made of synthetic materials. Wood, bamboo, cork, or a simple area rug are also good options.

HIGH-EFFICIENCY AIR PURIFIER
These filters help purify the air and can remove 99.97 percent particles bigger than 0.3 micron in diameter.

PAINTING
Replace solvent-based paints with low-VOC or zero-VOC paints.

BEDDING
Hypoallergenic bedding and mattress can be used to curtail contaminants.

UNSCENTED
Avoid the use of scented items, like candles, dryer sheets, air fresheners, etc.

FURNITURE
is a source of a variety of VOCs, especially pressed wood and plastics. Look for items that are Greenguard certified.

CARPET
Keep carpet in your nursery to a minimum as carpet can trap dust mites, pollen, animal dander, and mold spores, and can emit (or "off-gas") harmful VOCs.

TIPS ABOUT VOCs

WELCOME TO THE WORLD
WHAT HAPPENS RIGHT AFTER BIRTH

As soon as baby is born there are several procedures that will take place. Here is a list of the things that you can expect to occur.

CORD CLAMPING

Once baby is delivered, the umbilical cord is clamped near the belly button and a little farther up the cord, and then cut. This ends baby's dependence on the mom for oxygen and nutrition.

Delayed Clamping

In delayed cord clamping, the umbilical cord isn't clamped immediately at birth. Instead, it's clamped and cut 30 seconds to one minute after birth, allowing the blood supply from the placenta to flow to the baby.

Benefits of delayed clamping:

- Increases hemoglobin levels
- Increases neonatal blood volume
- Increases iron stores
- Increases stem cell levels
- Increases myelin in the baby's brain
- Boosts baby's immune system
- May reduce the need for blood transfusion in premature babies

Consult your doctor to see if delayed cord clamping is right for you and your baby.

CORD CUTTING

After being clamped, the cord is cut by your doctor or birthing partner, leaving behind a stump.

APGAR TEST

Between one and five minutes after birth, the Apgar test is performed. This is a scoring system to evaluate the condition of a newborn.

Apgar stands for: Appearance (skin color),

Pulse (heart rate),

Grimace Response (reflexes),

Activity (muscle tone),

Respiration (breathing rate and effort).

Each of the five conditions is scored 0, 1, or 2.

SKIN-TO-SKIN: AFTER VAGINAL BIRTH

If your baby is healthy and you want immediate skin-to-skin contact, your doctor will lay the baby on mom's bare chest right after delivery. Baby can stay there for most of the post-delivery routine.

SKIN-TO-SKIN: AFTER C-SECTION BIRTH

If baby is delivered by C-section, he may have amniotic fluid in his lungs. The doctor will assess this, and if everything is OK, she will give baby to the parents for skin-to-skin contact.

BABY MEASUREMENTS

A nurse will record the baby's official weight, head circumference, and body length. The nurse will also make a copy of baby's handprint and footprint, and give baby a bath if the parents agree.

Delayed bathing: The World Health Organization recommends delaying the first bath until at least 24 hours after birth. Babies are born covered in a natural white substance called vernix, which has antibacterial and healing properties.

VITAMIN K

Baby gets a Vitamin K injection to help with blood clotting and prevent bleeding.

EYE DROPS

Antibiotic ointment is routinely put in the eyes of newborns to prevent neonatal conjunctivitis (pink eye). This condition is more likely when the mother has a history of chlamydia or gonorrhea. The eye ointment also kills germs but is specifically used to prevent blindness caused by STDs.

CORD BLOOD & TISSUE BANK

Cord blood and tissue banking is the process of saving the remaining blood in the umbilical cord or cord tissue for potential future use.

WHAT IS CORD BLOOD BANKING?

It is the collection and storage of blood from the umbilical cord at birth. The umbilical cord blood contains blood-forming stem cells, which are potentially useful for treating conditions of the blood and immune system.

The fluid is easy to collect and has more stem cells than those collected from bone marrow.

If an immediate family member has a disease that requires a bone marrow transplant, cord blood from a newborn child may have the potential to be a treatment for the genetic parents and the siblings.

TYPES OF CORD BLOOD BANKS

Public Banking

Organizations that store donated cord blood for other sick children and research. This blood is available to anyone.

Private Banking

Cord blood banks that store your baby's cord blood for your family for an annual fee.

WHAT IS CORD TISSUE BANKING?

This process preserves a segment of your baby's umbilical cord, which can contain millions of stem cells of various kinds that can develop into tissue to form the nervous system, sensory organs, circulatory tissues, skin, bone, and cartilage.

These cells can be preserved for future use to potentially treat diseases and medical conditions.

WHAT TO KNOW

If you are interested in banking either cord blood or tissue, you will need to plan ahead to do this.

Currently, cord blood and tissue banking isn't routine in hospitals or home deliveries. You will need to notify your doctor and hospital before the birth that you are interested in banking.

You will also need to have received the cord blood kit that is ordered ahead of time from the cord blood bank you have chosen. You will bring that kit to the hospital when you go in for delivery.

Once the blood/tissue is collected, you will need to notify the bank that it is ready for pickup and transport to the bank.

NEWBORN HOSPITAL SCREENINGS

There are several tests done while you are in the hospital with your newborn. These tests are routine and help health professionals identify and treat specific conditions.

SCREENING REQUIREMENTS

All states require screenings to be performed on newborns. Any decision to decline testing should first be discussed with your doctor, since newborn screenings are designed to protect the health of the baby.

Even babies who are not born in a hospital need to have a newborn screening performed. If a home birth is planned, the licensed midwife may be qualified to complete the newborn blood test and hearing screening; if not, this will need to be arranged by your pediatrician.

PREEMIE BABY SCREENINGS

Babies born premature, with health conditions or with a low birth weight, often have certain medical problems that require special treatments. These treatments can affect the screening results, requiring a special process and more than one blood draw throughout baby's hospital stay.

BLOOD TEST HEEL STICK

The heel of the newborn is pricked and drops of blood are placed on a filter paper, which is sent to the lab.

Here are some disorders that are screened for:

- Phenylketonuria (PKU)
- Cystic fibrosis
- Congenital hypothyroidism
- Maple syrup urine disease
- Sickle cell disease
- Galactosemia
- Homocystinuria
- Congenital Adrenal Hyperplasia

HEARING SCREEN

Two tests can be used to screen for hearing loss in babies:

1. Otoacoustic Emission Test
Determines how the baby's ears respond to sound. A small earpiece or probe is placed in the baby's ear and sounds are played. When hearing is normal, sound waves travel back through the ear canal. These are measured by the earpiece. If no echo is detected, that can indicate potential hearing loss.

2. Auditory Brain Stem Response
This test evaluates the brain's response to sound. During this test, miniature earphones are placed in the ears and sounds are played. Electrodes placed on baby's scalp track and measure the brain's response to those sounds, determining if there is any hearing loss.

PULSE OXIMETRY TEST

Measures how much oxygen is in the blood.

Sensors are placed on the baby's hand or foot to measure the heart rate and blood oxygen level.

Low blood oxygen levels can identify babies who may have Critical Congenital Heart Disease (CCHD). The test is painless and takes a few minutes, typically done when the baby is at least 24 hours of age.

PEDIATRICIAN
FINDING A DOCTOR FOR BABY

Your baby's first examination may be with a hospital pediatrician or your chosen pediatrician. It depends on the hospital's policy and whether your newborn's doctor makes rounds there. If a hospital pediatrician checks your baby, you should have those notes sent to your pediatrician.

WHAT IS A PEDIATRICIAN?

Pediatricians are doctors who manage the health of infants, children, and adolescents. They treat children with issues ranging from minor illnesses to serious health concerns. Pediatricians also handle growth and development issues. They are the first people to call whenever your child is sick.

After you leave the hospital, your pediatrician will typically see your baby 48 to 72 hours later. She will see your child many times from birth to age two. Starting at ages two or three, your pediatrician will likely see your child once a year.

WHAT DO PEDIATRICIANS DO?

- Perform physical exams
- Track your baby's progress in reaching developmental milestones
- Administer vaccinations
- Prescribe medications and treatments
- Diagnose illnesses, infections, and injuries
- Provide advice regarding child's physical, emotional, and social development
- Answer any questions regarding growth and development
- Connect you with other pediatric specialists if needed

FINDING A PEDIATRICIAN

One of the biggest decisions to make before your baby arrives is selecting a pediatrician. It's important to have a pediatrician that you feel comfortable with before the baby is born, because after your baby is born, you will be too busy to look for a doctor.

1. Ask Friends, Family, and Colleagues

Start by asking your friends and family for their recommendations and compile a list.

2. Choose Someone Close to Home

You will want the office to be close to your home, as you will be going there a lot at first.

3. Check Your Insurance

Check that the doctor is accepting new patients and can take your insurance.

4. Arrange a Visit

Once you have decided on a couple of doctors you like, you will want to schedule a meeting with the doctor and visit their office. Ask up front if there is any charge for this meeting.

5. Prepare Questions

When you meet with the pediatrician, you should be ready with a list of questions that pertain to you and topics of interest like:

- Breastfeeding vs. formula?
- Circumcision vs. no circumcision?
- Vaccinations?
- Is the doctor board certified?
- Is the doctor an American Academy of Pediatrics (AAP) member?
- Is the doctor available by phone and/or email after hours?
- Check the state's medical board website to see if there have been any complaints filed

Either you run
the day or the day
runs you.

THE SIMPLEST BABY PLAN

Scheduling techniques that will help you regain control and find more joy with your baby

WHY A SCHEDULE

A schedule is a must-have that benefits both you and baby

Having a new baby can create an overwhelming sense of chaos. In order to regain some degree of control, getting your baby on a day-and-night schedule is essential. Being on a schedule establishes a routine that can help your baby reach various milestones, such as sleeping through the night.

For some parents, having a routine may feel too restrictive, and they may want to go with what they feel is right for them and their baby. It does take commitment to stay on a schedule, but it has been our experience that a schedule is a huge life changer.

An age-appropriate day schedule helps baby not get overtired or overstimulated. A schedule will help parents plan the day and its activities.

SLEEPING ALL NIGHT

Reaching this holy grail is the goal of all parents, and getting on a schedule can help you achieve it.

WHAT IS A BABY SCHEDULE?

A set time for baby routines and activities:

1 EATING

2 PLAYING

3 SLEEPING

CAN BREASTFEEDING MOMS BE ON A SCHEDULE?

Yes, being on a schedule will help eliminate guessing when to feed next. It can also help babies become stronger breastfeeders as they learn to take in full meals instead of small snacks throughout the day and night.

THE BENEFITS OF A SCHEDULE

- It makes life easier.
- It's comforting to baby.
- It moves you faster toward having baby sleep through the night.
- It provides predictable sleeping and feeding habits.
- It provides parents a greater sense of control.
- It makes it easier for others to step in and help out.
- It helps prevent baby becoming overtired and overstimulated.

SCHEDULING MISTAKES

Being inconsistent

Changing the routine or not sticking to it is a sure way for it not to work. Big changes in a schedule, like missing a nap or feeding, are sure to create a very unhappy baby. Babies learn to anticipate the next step in a schedule, and when that routine gets messed up, everything falls apart.

Keeping baby awake too long

Keeping baby up too long is a surefire way to create an overstimulated baby, which will negatively affect the schedule and sleeping.

THE SIMPLEST BABY PLAN
HOW IT WORKS

LOGS & SCHEDULES

There is a log and schedule for:

- Month 1
- 3 Weeks to 3 Months
- 3 Months to 6 Months
- 6 Months to 12 Months

SCHEDULE TRACKING

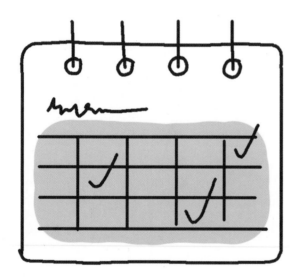

The schedule tracks and logs specific baby activities.

- When to feed and how much
- When to play
- When to sleep and how much
- Peeing
- Pooping
- Note any issues or fussiness
- Note any medications used
- When to bathe

It's important to understand that all babies are different, so you may need to be flexible on the specific scheduled times for your baby.

GO WITH YOUR BABY'S FLOW

FIRST MONTH LOG

During baby's first month there really is no set schedule other than waking baby up about every three hours for feeding. The most important thing for baby at this time is to have healthy weight gain. Your doctor and you will track your baby's weight and development to ensure her health progress.

You will use the Simplest Baby Log during the day and night to note all your baby's activities.

SIMPLEST BABY LOG   DATE: 11/26 night

START TIME	END TIME	TOTAL SLEEP	TOTAL FEED TIME	FEEDING AMOUNT	BREAST STARTED WITH R	BREAST STARTED WITH L	PEE	POOP	NOTES
8:30	9:45	1:15			○	○			
9:45	10:30		45	3 oz	○	○	×		Gassy
10:30	12:45	2:15			○	○			
12:45	1:30		45	3.3 oz	○	○	×		
1:30	3:45	2:15			○	○			
3:45	4:30		45	3.2 oz	○	○	×	×	
4:30	6:45	2:15			○	○			
6:45					○	○	×	2×	
					○	○			
					○	○			
					○	○			
					○	○			
					○	○			
					○	○			
TOTALS				9.5 oz					

SCHEDULES

SCHEDULES

During the day you will follow the Simplest Baby day plan that matches your baby's age:

- **3 Week to 3 Month Schedule**
- **3–6 Month Schedule**
- **6–12 Month Schedule**

During the night you will continue to use the Simplest Baby Log.

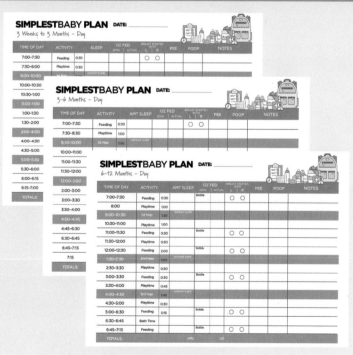

SCHEDULES & LOGS

All schedules and logs can be found in the back of this book, or you can go to Simplestbaby.com to download the free Simplest Baby Plan forms.

SCHEDULES
HOW THEY WORK

SIMPLESTBABY PLAN   DATE:

3-6 Months - Day

TIME OF DAY	ACTIVITY	AMT SLEEP		OZ FE
			GOAL	
7:00-7:30	Feeding	0:30		
7:30-8:30	Playtime	1:00		
8:30-10:00	1st Nap	1:30	AMOUNT SLEEP	

SCHEDULE
Pick the schedule that matches your child's age: newborn, 3–6 weeks, 3–6 months, or 6–12 months.

DAILY TIMES
Follow each step hour by hour.

ACTIVITIES
Activities are outlined for the day by time. As you reach the listed times, you simply follow the activities that correspond to that time.

FEEDING & FOOD
Track the amount of food you intended for baby to eat and what your baby actually ate.

DAYTIME

During the day, you will be using one of the daytime schedules to track all the various activities of your baby.

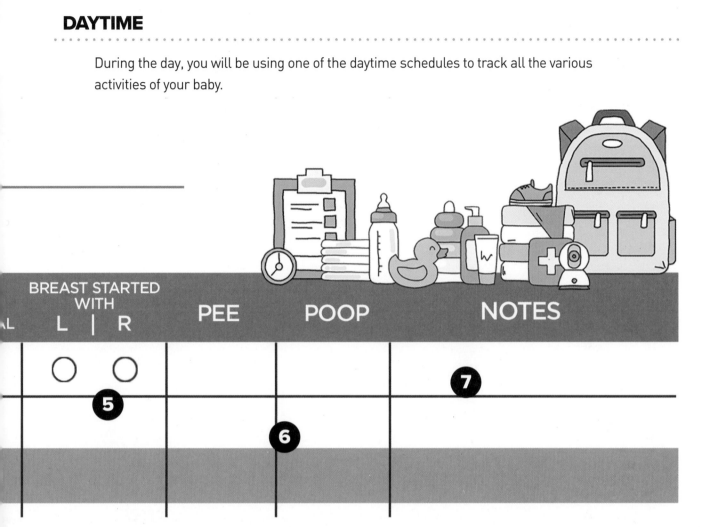

BREAST STARTED WITH		PEE	POOP	NOTES
L	R			

BREASTFEEDING

You will track which breast you started with at your last feeding so that you can be sure to start with the opposite at the next feeding.

PEE & POOP

Check these boxes each time your baby pees or poops.

NOTES

This area is where you will jot down notes regarding baby's fussiness, gas, constipation, sleep patterns, or any other issues.

NIGHTTIME

During the night, you will use the Simplest Baby Log to record all activities that happen throughout the night.

A bottle of
the house
white please.

TIME TO EAT

What you need to know about feeding your baby and the needed essentials

FEEDING MILESTONES
WHEN TO START FEEDING AND WHAT

While every baby is different, the stages outlined here provide a general guideline for when babies start each feeding milestone. Instead of starting each stage at the ages listed, it is usually more important that your baby moves through the different stages when he is ready.

FEEDING MILESTONES

AGE	MEAL TYPE

Breast milk or formula will be a primary part of the nutritional needs of baby in every stage of feeding for the first year.

0–4 MONTHS

BREAST MILK OR FORMULA ONLY

Feed your baby exclusively breast milk or formula; no solid foods.

4–6 MONTHS

ADD PUREE | STAGE 1

If baby can sit up well in a high chair, support his head, and shows interest in your food, it might be time to try feeding baby his first solids. Single-ingredient foods like oatmeal, barley, and pureed fruits or vegetables should be baby's first solid foods.

6–8 MONTHS

ADD THICKER PUREE | STAGE 2

At eight months, you can begin to introduce thicker purees and soft finger foods: options that include single ingredients and purees of a combination of foods.

1 YEAR

MORE SOLIDS | STAGE 3

At about 12 months, introduce foods that have more texture and small chunks to encourage baby to chew. You can also introduce finger foods at this time.

BREAST MILK VS. FORMULA

The decision to breastfeed or use formula is a personal one, and can depend on many factors, comfort level, lifestyle, or medical issues. Breastfeeding or formula feeding is a choice all parents should get to make for themselves, guilt free.

BREAST MILK

Breast milk is truly amazing and ultimately baby's best source of nutrition. The fats in breast milk are essential to brain development, vitamin absorption, and helping your baby gain weight. Breast milk is full of vitamins and infection-fighting antibodies. The proteins, calcium, and iron in breast milk are easily absorbed by babies.

Although health experts believe breast milk is the best nutritional choice for infants, breastfeeding is not always possible.

FORMULA

Formula is a manufactured food for feeding babies. It comes as either a powder or a premixed liquid. Today's formulas are a healthy alternative to breast milk, providing many of the nutrients your baby needs to grow and thrive.

Choosing the right formula is important and something to be discussed with your pediatrician.

FEEDING AND BONDING

Some parents worry that if they don't breastfeed, they won't bond with their baby. But loving parents will always create a bond with their children.

WHAT IS IN THEM?

BREAST MILK

- **Antibodies** to fight against viruses and bacteria

- **White blood cells** to fight infection and help protect against illness and disease

- **Hormones** that positively affect baby's growth and development

- **Stem cells** that can be used in the body's development

- **Probiotics** that support a healthy digestive and immune system

- **Fatty acids | DHA, ARA** for development of the nervous system and body organs

- A healthy mix of **vitamins, proteins, and fat**

VS.

FORMULA

Ingredients for formulas vary by manufacturer. Below is a list of the most common ingredients.

- **Whey and/or casein protein** for supporting growth and development

- **Vegetable oils** as a fat source

- **Fatty acids | DHA, ARA**, derived from fish oil or algae to support brain and nervous system development

- Essential **vitamins and minerals** from plant and animal sources

- Carbohydrates usually derived from **lactose** for energy and growth

- **Probiotics** for digestive and immune system health

- **Prebiotics** to support a healthy digestive and immune system

THE MUST-HAVES
FOR BREASTFEEDING

3 NURSING BRAS | NURSING TANK TOPS

A quality bra or nursing tank top is essential for comfort and support. Look for soft, stretchy fabric that has a cup that gives: one that allows easy access to your breast without needing to remove your bra.

8–12 NURSING PADS

Look for ones that are soft, absorbent, and made of cotton. Having a ready supply of absorbent nursing pads to tuck inside your bra is important. Pads come in three types: disposable pads, reusable cotton pads, or silicone pads.

1 NIPPLE CREAM

Look for natural, hypoallergenic, plant-based nipple cream that has no parabens, no mineral oil, no petroleum, and no fragrance. Avoid nipple balms that contain alcohol. Look for nursing balms that have a nurturing blend of natural ingredients like shea butter, olive and argan oil, and calendula extract to help nourish your skin and prevent it from chapping.

1 NURSING PILLOW

Look for a pillow that wraps around your waist and that you can rest your arms on while nursing. Look for one that is easy to clean and has a removable cover that can be washed.

2–3 SLEEP BRAS

Rather than back clasps that may be uncomfortable to lie on, sleep bras have either front closures or pull-aside cups with no clasps in front or back. This makes lounging and sleeping much more comfortable while still offering gentle support for your breasts.

1 BREAST PUMP

There are different types of breast pumps available depending on how often you need to pump. You can buy your own or rent one. See the section on breast pumps.

1–2 BOXES OF MILK STORAGE BAGS

These bags and containers are specially made for the collection and storage of breast milk. They are necessities for anyone who plans on pumping their milk. These products are designed to withstand freezing and thawing, and they can safely store your milk for long periods of time. A box may contain 50–100 bags.

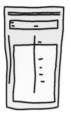

3–4 NIPPLE SHIELDS

This breastfeeding accessory is used if you are having a difficult time getting a good latch or if your nipples need protection while healing. These flexible silicone covers fit over the nipple and areola. To work effectively, they need to be sized properly for both your nipple as well as your baby's mouth.

1–2 NURSING COVER-UPS

Nursing cover-ups, ponchos, or scarves are articles of clothing that can be held in place around your neck while covering your chest area for discreet breastfeeding in public.

1 COOLER

If you are going to be pumping at work, you will need a cooler to keep the milk cold and transport it home.

GET THE RIGHT STUFF!
Go to Simplestbaby.com for recommendations of the smartest baby products and essentials.

BREASTFEEDING
KEY THINGS TO KNOW

Breastfeeding is a wonderful thing to be able to do for your baby, but not everyone is comfortable or successful doing so. Whether you do or don't—as well as the length of time—is a personal choice, and you should never feel guilty whatever you decide.

WHAT IS IT?

Breastfeeding, also referred to as nursing, is the process of feeding babies with milk from the mammary glands (a woman's breasts). This is done by baby feeding directly on the breast or from a bottle of milk expressed from the breast by a pump.

COLOSTRUM: first milk or liquid gold
This nutrient-rich yellow breast fluid that is produced immediately following birth is tremendously good for baby, loaded with antibodies and nutrients that fight infection and disease and promote immunity and growth.

It is produced for only a short time. In two to three days, your regular breast milk, which is whiter and creamier than colostrum, will start.

WHY DO IT?

Breast milk is an amazing food for babies. Health experts and the AAP recommend breastfeeding all infants because of its many health benefits for baby and mother.

Health Benefits for Baby
Helps prevent: diabetes
childhood cancers
obesity
infections
diarrhea
respiratory infections
asthma

Health Benefits for Mom
Helps burn calories
Lowers risk of ovarian cancer
Lowers risk of osteoporosis

WHEN AND HOW LONG?

It is recommended that mothers begin breastfeeding in the first hour of a baby's life. The American Academy of Pediatrics (AAP) recommends mothers continue breastfeeding for at least the first year of baby's life or, at a minimum, the first six months.

FIRST FEEDINGS

20–45
Minutes

15 Minutes
each breast

When you start breastfeeding, it will take 20–45 minutes, about 15 minutes on each side. Make sure baby spends quality time on each breast. To start with, you will be nursing frequently, around 8–12 times a day.

QUICK TIP
Always wash your breast before breastfeeding. Some babies don't like sour smells or the taste of nipple cream.

BREASTFEEDING LATCH

Learning to successfully breastfeed and getting a good latch with your baby is important. It also can be challenging, so be patient.

QUICK TIP
Breastfeeding Should Not Hurt!
A correct latch is important. While in the hospital, take advantage of the nurses and lactation consultants who can help you and baby perfect the latch.

WHAT IS A LATCH?

Latch describes how the baby's mouth attaches to the breast while breastfeeding.

HOW IT WORKS

A good latch will promote quality milk flow and reduces nipple discomfort, while a poor latch can cause low milk flow, gassiness, low weight gain for baby, and blocked milk ducts for mom. With a good latch the nipple and a large portion of the areola will be in your baby's mouth.

CAUSES OF A BAD LATCH

- Size of your breasts and nipples
- How open the baby's mouth is
- Your comfort level
- Poor breastfeeding position
- Poor alignment
- The latch to the nipple is off-center
- Flat or inverted nipples
- Baby has a tongue tie
- Baby is premature

SORENESS

In the beginning, when you first start breastfeeding, some nipple soreness is normal. This usually subsides once your milk comes in and you and your baby become more accustomed to breastfeeding. Making sure you and baby are positioned correctly will promote a good latch and help prevent sore nipples.

If you have intense nipple pain or soreness, or you struggle to get a comfortable latch, it's best to get help from a breastfeeding professional, public-health nurse, lactation consultant, newborn-care specialist, your doctor, or midwife.

STEPS FOR GETTING A GOOD LATCH

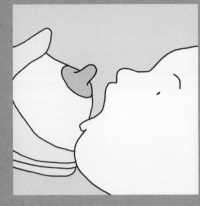

STEP 1

First position your baby so he is directly facing you, with his tummy against yours. Then slowly bring baby's chin to your breast.

STEP 2

Place your thumb and fingers around your areola and bring baby to your breast. Place the nipple between baby's upper lip and nose. Tilting back your baby's head slightly, tickle baby's upper lip with your nipple to encourage baby to widely open his mouth.

STEP 3

When your baby opens his mouth wide with the chin dropped and tongue down, you can begin putting your breast into baby's mouth. Begin by placing baby's lower jaw well below the nipple. The nipple should be angled towards the roof of baby's mouth.

STEP 4

Tilt baby's head forward, and roll the breast fully into baby's mouth. Baby's upper jaw should be deeply on the breast. Make sure baby takes the entire nipple and at least $1^{1/2}$ inches of the areola into the mouth. Be sure nothing is blocking baby's nose.

TOP BREASTFEEDING
POSITIONS

There are many different positions for breastfeeding. We have listed the top positions here. It should be noted that not every position works for everyone, so it's important to find the one that works best for you and your baby.

QUICK TIP

At every feeding you should start with the breast opposite the one you started to feed with the previous time.

#1 Position

CRADLE HOLD

This is one of the most common breastfeeding positions. Support your baby with the arm on the same side as the breast baby is feeding from, not the opposite arm. Your baby's head will be cradled in the crook of your arm near your elbow. Using a pillow for support can be helpful.

CROSS CRADLE HOLD

Bring baby across your body, so you are tummy to tummy. If baby is nursing on your left side, cradle the baby and support her neck with your right hand and arm. At the same time hold and present your breast with your left hand. Using a breastfeeding pillow when nursing in this position can make it easier and more comfortable. Good for newborns and young babies as it provides a bit more support.

Good for Newborns

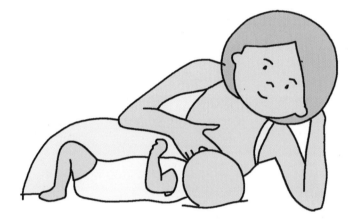

SIDE-LYING HOLD

You'll want to lie on your side, and face your baby toward your breast, making sure baby is supported with one hand. Use the other hand to take your breast and touch the nipple to your baby's lips. Once your baby latches on, you can then use one arm to support yourself and the other to hold your baby close.

FOOTBALL/RUGBY HOLD

If you're recovering from a C-section or if you have large breasts, the football hold may be an easier position to maintain as it keeps your baby's weight off your abdomen. With your elbow bent, hold your baby beside you, level with your waist. Support your baby's head with an open hand and face baby toward your breast. Baby's back will rest on your forearm, just like holding a football.

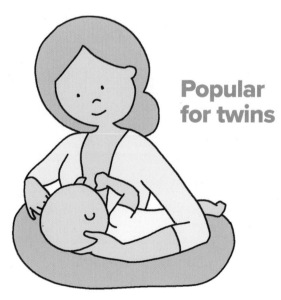

Popular for twins

BOOSTING & IMPROVING BREAST MILK

MORE MILK, PLEASE

OMEGA-3s

These are crucial building blocks for the growth of neural and vision cells during the first two years of baby's life. While DHA is naturally occurring in breast milk, moms can boost the amount available to baby by consuming more fish, especially salmon. Make sure the salmon is wild, not farm raised. If you're not big on seafood, you can take a 200- to 300-milligram supplement per day.

EAT RIGHT

Certain foods have been used to increase the flow of breast milk. Oatmeal is the most common, and along with flax seeds and brewer's yeast, oatmeal is often the main ingredient in lactation cookies, which you can either buy or make yourself. Other foods known to increase milk supply include almonds, barley, fennel, and fenugreek.

PROBIOTICS

Many babies lack good bacteria in their guts that help them digest breast milk and protect them from potentially harmful bacteria linked to colic, eczema, and allergies. Probiotics also support baby's metabolism and immune system, building the foundation for good health that can last a lifetime.

NURSE OR PUMP OFTEN

You can increase your milk supply by feeding or pumping as often as you can: every two to three hours during baby's first few weeks. If you need more help boosting supply, consider pumping after breastfeeding for 10–15 minutes. This technique tricks your body into thinking that it needs to produce more milk.

DRINK MORE WATER AND GET MORE REST

Hydrate, hydrate, hydrate. Staying well hydrated is very important for milk production. You are the sole source of hydration for your baby, so you are drinking for two. Getting enough rest is also critical to improving milk production.

PUMPING
INTRODUCTION

Choosing a breast pump can be a confusing decision. It is actually very specific to each person's situation. There is no way for someone to know ahead of time what their milk supply is going to be and how they will respond to a certain pump.

If you have a pump and you are not getting good results, speak with a lactation consultant, who can help figure out if the problem is the pump or your milk supply.

WHY PUMP?

- You may want to store milk so others can feed baby any time you're sleeping or away—whether you're going back to work, running errands, taking a well-deserved break—or using medication that could affect baby.

- Your baby is unable to latch or feed directly from the breast.

- You want to give your baby breast milk but don't want to feed directly from the breast.

- You plan on donating milk to a milk bank or milk-exchange program.

- You're trying to increase your milk supply and need to alleviate pressure or you are suffering from mastitis and need to drain your breast to help healing.

QUICK TIP

If your hospital permits, bring your clean pump with you to the hospital. The doctor will often have you start pumping to get the milk flowing while there.

RENTAL PUMPS	PURCHASED PUMPS

RENTAL PUMPS

- Have hospital-grade motors that will pump more milk in less time

- Quieter

- Can help increase your supply

- Can be helpful when pumping for several babies, a preemie, or a baby who is having difficulty breastfeeding

- Somewhat bulky and heavy

- Cost about $50 per month

- Can be easily returned if pumping doesn't work for you

VS.

PURCHASED PUMPS

- $50 for a hand pump
  $250–$400 for a high-quality pump
  $1,000 for a hospital-grade pump

- If you plan on pumping for a longer period of time or you plan on using it for several children, it might be a more efficient investment

- Lightweight and easy to carry

- Better for only occasional pumping

ADDITIONAL THINGS TO CONSIDER

DON'T BUY OR BORROW SOMEONE ELSE'S PUMP

Due to the risk of cross contamination, it is best not to borrow a pump or use a secondhand pump. (Hospital-grade rentals are built with protective barriers and approved by the FDA for multiple users.)

INSURANCE

Check your insurance policy: it may pay for some of the pump rental or purchase cost, especially if you or baby has a condition that makes breastfeeding difficult.

PUMPING
GETTING THINGS FLOWING

Knowing when, how much, and how to keep things flowing are among the most common questions new moms ask. Much depends on you and your baby; some moms begin soon after birth but others wait a couple of weeks.

WHEN TO START

Healthy Baby:

If your baby is healthy, has good weight gain, and you will not be away from your baby during feeding times, you can wait to begin pumping four to six weeks.

Premature, Ill, or Special-Needs Babies:

Should your baby not be able to feed right away or have a low birth weight, it is recommended that you begin pumping soon after birth.

Babies That Are Separated from Mom:

If you have to be separated from your baby, it can be helpful to begin pumping and storing your breast milk so it is available to others who might be feeding your baby.

Going Back to Work:

If you are planning on going back to work, it is recommended that you begin pumping and storing milk several weeks before.

TIPS FOR PUMPING

1. Pump in the morning; moms tend to get the most milk at this time.
2. Pump after nursing to fully empty the breasts.
3. Using the right size flange for your nipple size is important.
4. Plan to pump eight to ten times in 24 hours.
5. Pumping both breasts at the same time increases milk production.

HELPFUL TIPS FOR PUMPING

1. Read up on the basics of breast pumping; be sure to review your breast pump instructions.

2. Relax and find a quiet, comfortable place to pump.

3. Have a drink and a snack with you.

4. If your pump is battery operated, charge your pump and make sure it is working.

5. Always wash your hands with soap and water before pumping.

6. Make sure the cup of the pump has a good seal over the breast.

7. Start with low suction and increase it as milk begins to flow.

8. Encourage letdown by gently massaging your breast or using a warm compress.

STORING BREAST MILK

WHERE	TEMPERATURE	HOW LONG WILL IT LAST
Sitting out	Room temperature	5–6 hours
Refrigerator	40°F	5–6 days
Freezer	0°F	6–12 months
In a cooler	Ice packed	24 hours

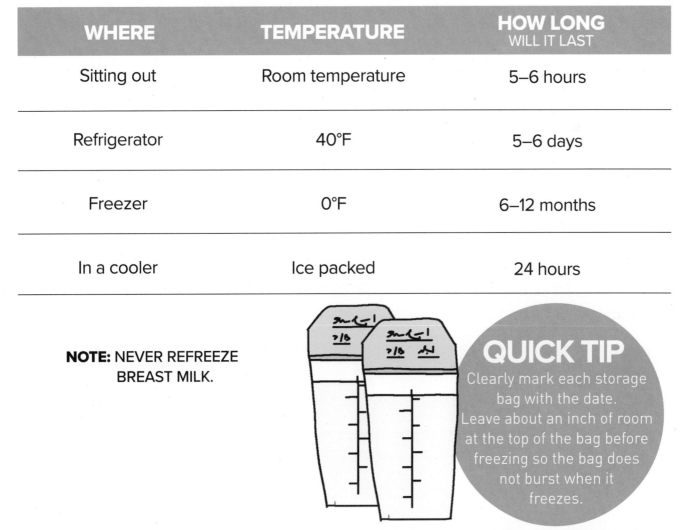

NOTE: NEVER REFREEZE BREAST MILK.

QUICK TIP
Clearly mark each storage bag with the date. Leave about an inch of room at the top of the bag before freezing so the bag does not burst when it freezes.

POWER PUMPING
BOOSTING MILK SUPPLY

QUICK TIP

It might be helpful to consult a lactation specialist or your pediatrician for guidance and assistance before power pumping.

WHAT IS IT?

Power pumping is a breastfeeding method that is used to increase a mother's milk supply.

It involves frequent on and off pumping that mimics cluster feeding, which is when baby nurses in short bursts several times an hour. This naturally signals the body to produce more milk to keep up with baby's needs.

WHY DO IT?

If you are mostly nursing or pumping exclusively and your milk production seems to have slowed down, power pumping can provide a boost.

SIGNS OF DECREASED MILK SUPPLY

- Baby isn't gaining weight
- Baby is losing weight.
- Baby isn't having enough wet and dirty diapers.

HOW IT WORKS?

You will need to dedicate at least an hour a day for a week to power pumping. Power pumping is done in addition to your normal pumping/nursing routine. You can replace one of your regular pumping sessions with a power pumping session. Some women power pump both breasts simultaneously or one at a time, depending on their pump.

HOW OFTEN SHOULD ONE POWER PUMP?

Once or twice a day.

TIPS FOR POWER PUMPING

Manual vs. Electric Pumps

You can use a manual or electric pump, but you might find an electric pump easier due to the frequency of pumping.

Understand Milk Production

Before beginning, it's important to be clear on why your milk production has decreased. Is your pump working correctly? Is baby latching correctly?

Hands-Free Pumping Bra

Consider getting a hands-free pumping bra, as it might make things a bit easier, more comfortable, and free your hands for other activities.

Relax

Find a calm, quiet, comfortable place to pump—it helps the milk letdown.

Be Aware of Your Breast

Overpumping or overly strong suction can cause damage to your breast, negatively impacting your pumping.

Overpumping

If you are not having a milk supply problem, you should not be power pumping. Unnecessary power pumping can create an oversupply, resulting in engorged breasts, mastitis, or other issues.

TYPICAL
POWER PUMPING SCHEDULE

PUMP: **20** minutes

REST: **10** minutes

PUMP: **20** minutes

REST: **10** minutes

PUMP: **10** minutes

*This is the schedule for each breast. This means that if you do each breast separately, it will require around two hours. If you have a pump that allows you to pump both breasts simultaneously, then it will be an hour total.

PROTECT THE BREAST

F#@K, BREASTFEEDING CAN BE A PAIN

You are not alone if you are experiencing discomfort or challenges while breastfeeding; it is very common. Just because you are a woman does not mean it is going to be easy or come naturally.

SIMPLE SOLUTIONS FOR COMMON NURSING ISSUES

Many early breastfeeding difficulties can be dealt with by making simple adjustments.

- Change baby's feeding position.

- Completely drain each breast.

- Nurse for 15–20 minutes on one breast before switching.

- Feed frequently to prevent engorgement.

- Alternate the breast you offer first at each feeding.

- Take steps to heal sore or cracked nipples.

- Make sure your bra is not too tight.

The information provided is not a substitute for professional medical advice, diagnosis, or treatment. Always consult your pediatrician or health-care provider to ensure that a treatment is right for you and your child.

7 TIPS TO SOOTHE SORE BREASTS

 Use moist heat on your breasts for a few minutes or take a brief hot shower before breastfeeding. This may help the milk begin to flow. Note: Use of heat for extended periods of time (more than five minutes) may make swelling worse.

 Use cold compresses for 10 minutes after feedings to reduce swelling.

 Gently massage and compress the breast when the baby pauses between sucks. This may help drain the breast, leaving less milk behind.

 Ask your health-care professional about medications such as ibuprofen to reduce pain and inflammation.

Consider getting a well-fitted, supportive nursing bra.

 Gently massage the breasts, which may help improve milk flow and reduce the discomfort of engorgement.

Hand expression or brief use of a breast pump may help soften the nipple and areola so that the baby can get a better latch.

QUICK TIP

When removing the breast from baby's mouth, don't just pull it out. Using a clean finger, insert it into baby's mouth between their gums to break the suction. When baby opens the mouth, keeping your finger between the gums, slowly remove the breast.

BREASTFEEDING
WHAT COULD GO WRONG?

Many of the issues relating to breastfeeding come from poor latching. When things do go wrong, they can result in some painful conditions.

THRUSH

WHAT IS IT?

Thrush is a yeast infection of the nipple that is not harmful but is painful. Thrush is caused by an overgrowth of the fungus candida in your baby's mouth. You can continue breastfeeding during an outbreak of thrush, but if your baby's mouth is sore, she may avoid latching or be reluctant to feed. Both you and your baby need to be treated for thrush if you have it; contact your doctor for treatment.

SYMPTOMS

- **Breast and nipple pain**: burning, itching, sharp stabbing pain
- **Swelling and redness** of the nipple and areola
- **Shiny or flaky nipples**: small blisters or white patches on nipples
- **White spots** in baby's mouth and on baby's tongue

TREATMENT & PREVENTION

- Use antifungal medication for you and your baby.
- Sterilize bottles, nipples, and pacifiers daily.
- Practice breast hygiene: change your breast pads and bras often if wet.
- Add probiotics to your and baby's diet.
- Air-dry nipples after feeding.
- Keep your hands clean.

The information provided is not a substitute for professional medical advice, diagnosis, or treatment. Always consult your pediatrician or health-care provider to ensure that a treatment is right for you and your child.

BLOCKED DUCTS

WHAT ARE THEY?

Breasts are made up of several mammary glands and ducts that carry milk to the nipple. When milk flow is obstructed, it can be due to a blocked milk duct. This can result in a painful buildup of milk and a lump the size of a pea or blueberry in the area of that blocked gland. The cause of blocked ducts is most likely a result of insufficiently draining the breast. Consult your doctor.

SYMPTOMS

- Pain in a specific location in the breast
- A swollen, tender lump in the breast
- A hot, swollen breast
- Decreased or slowing milk flow from one breast
- Lumpy area of the breast
- A small white blister on the nipple

TREATMENT & PREVENTION

- Apply heat to the breast.
- Nurse more on affected breast.
- Soak breast in Epsom salts.
- Wear loose-fitting clothing.
- Don't wear an underwire bra.
- Pump after the baby has fed.
- Fully drain the breast when feeding.
- Change feeding position.
- Take ibuprofen for pain.
- Gently massage your breasts before and during nursing.

BREASTFEEDING
WHAT COULD GO WRONG?
Continued

CRACKED NIPPLES

WHAT IS IT?

A condition that can occur in breastfeeding women in which the nipple develops a cut across the tip that may extend to its base. This can cause severe pain during breastfeeding and is a common result of a poor latch during feeding.

SYMPTOMS

- Breast and nipple irritation and pain
- Bleeding nipple
- A sore, dry, cracked nipple

TREATMENTS & PREVENTION

- Latch correctly.
- Use the proper feeding position.
- Apply breast milk to the nipple.
- Apply a warm compress.
- Rinse with saltwater.
- Apply 100 percent lanolin ointment.

- Change nursing pads frequently.
- Avoid friction on the nipple by not wearing bras that are too tight.
- Speak to a lactation specialist.
- Take pain medication: ibuprofen (Advil, Motrin) or acetaminophen (Tylenol).
- Protect nipples when removing them from baby's mouth with your finger.

The information provided is not a substitute for professional medical advice, diagnosis, or treatment. Always consult your pediatrician or health-care provider to ensure that a treatment is right for you and your child.

MASTITIS

WHAT IS IT?

Mastitis is inflammation of breast tissue that sometimes can involve an infection. It is usually caused by blocked breast ducts. It's important to contact your doctor if you develop any symptoms of a breast infection.

SYMPTOMS

- Breast and nipple pain and tenderness
- Redness and swelling
- Thickening of breast tissue, or a breast lump
- Continuous pain or continuous burning sensation while breastfeeding
- Feeling run-down and achy
- Low-grade fever of 101°F (38°C) or chills
- Severe cases: abscess or pus from nipple

TREATMENT & PREVENTION

- Get rest and drink plenty of water.
- Completely empty the breast.
- Change the breastfeeding position from one side to the other.
- Make sure your baby is latching properly.
- Alternately apply hot and cold compresses.
- Massage the breast lump.
- Nurse frequently.
- Take pain and anti-inflammatory medication.
- Take antibiotics.

THE MUST-HAVES
FOR BOTTLE FEEDING

5-8 BOTTLES

BPA-, BPS-, and phthalate-safe plastic bottles or glass bottles that have a venting anti-colic system designed to minimize air bubbles and help with reflux. Dishwasher safe with clear measurement markings. Silicone nipples are ideal as they are firmer, hold their shape longer, and are not damaged by heat.

5-10 BIBS

You will use a lot of bibs so look for easy-to-clean and comfortable, hypoallergenic bibs. Keep it simple—you may receive some very fancy bibs only to discover that simple is best.

5 BURP CLOTHS

100 percent hypoallergenic, superabsorbent, breathable organic cotton. They are made with soft organic fibers that are nontoxic and environmentally friendly.

1 BOTTLE WARMER

Not exactly a must-have, but you will need some way to warm up the milk. A steam bottle warmer can be very convenient. Make sure it is easy to clean, and heats safely and quickly.

1 DRYING RACK

This is something I didn't think I would need, but after buying one I had to admit it was helpful. If you choose to get one, it should be made from safe, nontoxic plastic and be free of lead, BPA, and phthalates.

FORMULA

If you are not breastfeeding, formula is a must-have to provide all the nutrition necessary for your baby during his first year. Like diapers, you will use a lot of it. Even if you are breastfeeding, you can use formula too.

Daddy Hack

BIBS: No need for fancy bibs if you want to save money. Simple white basic bibs with Velcro or snap closures work great.

BURP CLOTHS: Save some money by using a dish towel or clean cloth diaper. Also ask at the hospital if you can have one or two of the swaddles they use; they work great too.

GET THE RIGHT STUFF!

Go to Simplestbaby.com for recommendations of the smartest baby products and essentials.

BOTTLE FEEDING

MAKING SENSE OF BABY BOTTLES

Bottles come in different shapes and sizes, and with so many options on the market, it's hard to know what to use for your baby.

QUICK TIP

Some parents like to start with a smaller size bottle when baby is eating only a couple ounces and move to a larger size bottle when baby reaches six to nine ounces.

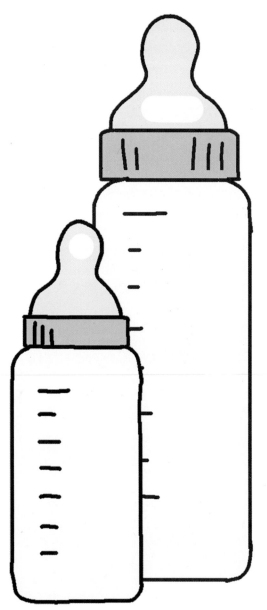

CHOOSING A BOTTLE

You may need to try several different bottle types to start with until you find one that works best for your baby.

BOTTLES TYPES

STANDARD BOTTLES: Traditional no-frills bottles in plastic, glass, and even stainless steel.

ANGLED-NECK BOTTLES: Bent at the neck to prevent air from filling the nipple, which may make for easier feedings and a less gassy baby.

DISPOSABLE-LINER BOTTLES: A hard shell bottle that holds an individual pouch of milk. The bag collapses as baby drinks, reducing gassiness.

WIDE-NECK BOTTLES: Short and squat, these bottles have a wide opening at the top with a wider nipple, making it similar to the breastfeeding experience. These are ideal for babies who get both breast and bottle feedings.

OUR RECOMMENDATION

VENTED BOTTLES: Bottles that include a built-in tube to prevent air pockets from forming in the bottle or nipple, helping to prevent gas.

CHOOSE THE RIGHT NIPPLE SIZES

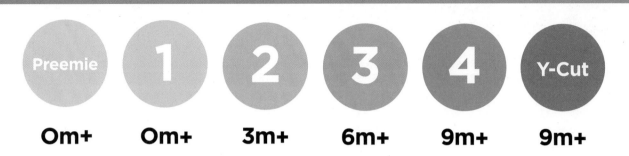

Preemie	1	2	3	4	Y-Cut
0m+	0m+	3m+	6m+	9m+	9m+

INCREASING MILK FLOW

As your baby grows you will be increasing the size of the nipple's hole that you use during feedings. The chart above shows a general time line for each nipple size. Each baby is different, and you will need to gauge what works best for your baby.

HOW MANY BOTTLES WILL YOU REALLY NEED?

2-3 Bottles   IF BREASTFEEDING

5-8 Bottles   IF BOTTLE FEEDING

WHAT TO LOOK FOR

#1 recommendation is to use glass bottles.

#2 recommendation is to use BPA-free plastic or eco-friendly bottles that are dishwasher safe and have a venting ability.

WASHING BOTTLES

The American Academy of Pediatrics recommends that a baby bottle be washed with hot water and soap and dried completely after every feeding. You can wash bottles by hand or in the dishwasher.

WARMING THINGS UP

WARMING UP THE MILK

Whether you use breast milk or formula, at some point you will need to warm it up.

QUICK TIP
Avoid overheating the milk to prevent the loss of nutrients.

The question is: Do you need a bottle warmer? The answer is: maybe. Originally, I was completely opposed to having a bottle warmer; I thought it was a waste of money. After using both the bottle warmer and the old-fashioned method of stovetop warming, I admit the bottle warmer is my go-to method for warming up milk. But if you are looking to save some money, the stovetop will do the trick.

BENEFITS OF BOTTLE WARMER:

- Consistent temperature
- Time efficient
- Convenient

THE RIGHT TEMP: 98.6°F | 37°C

A simple way to test the temperature of the milk is by sprinkling a few drops on the inside of your wrist. The milk is ready for the baby to drink when it feels lukewarm, **NOT HOT**.

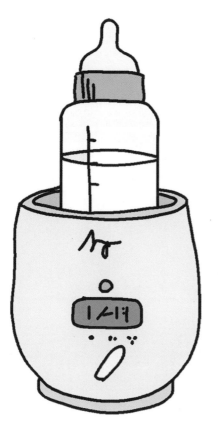

BOTTLE WARMERS

Both formula and breast milk can be warmed up in a bottle warmer. These devices make it quick and easy to heat milk thoroughly and evenly. Plus, there are no dishes to wash afterward.

GETTING THINGS WARMED UP

STOVETOP WARMING

A simple and inexpensive way to warm milk is by placing the bottle in a small pan of water on low heat. Every now and again, swirl the milk in the bottle and test its temperature on your wrist. The milk should be warm, not hot.

BOTTLE FEEDING

HOLD BABY; INSERT BOTTLE

It may sound like a simple thing, but there are some techniques that are worth knowing.

Daddy Hack

The bottle is for feeding; it is not a toy or a pacifier! Trust me, once the feeding is done, the bottle goes away. If you follow this rule, you will have a much easier time weaning the baby in the future.

3 BEST POSITIONS FOR BOTTLE FEEDING

POSITION 1
CRADLE HOLD

This is the standard method for holding a baby. Place the baby's head and body in the crook of your arm and wrap your hand around under your baby's bottom. Then, lift your elbow slightly to bring baby to an inclined position, with baby's head higher than baby's body.

As your baby grows and becomes more active, baby's flailing arms start getting in the way. There is a technique for getting them under control while using the cradle hold. I call it the tuck technique.

#1 Position for bottle feeding

CRADLE HOLD: TUCK TECHNIQUE
Getting control of those crazy little arms

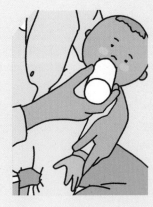

STEP #1:
While holding the baby cradled in your arms, tuck the baby's arm that is against your chest between the gap under your armpit. Arm number one is taken care of.

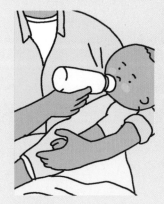

STEP #2:
Using the hand not holding the bottle, continue to cradle the baby while holding the baby's exposed hand/arm. You now control baby's other arm.

POSITION 2
LAP FEEDING

Sit down with your legs up and bent at the knees. Place baby with her back against your thighs, facing you, supporting the baby's head with your hand. Baby's feet and legs rest on your stomach.

POSITION 3
UPRIGHT FEEDING

More for babies who are slightly older and have more body control. Sit baby up on your lap and let his body rest against your chest or inside your arm. Can be helpful for babies who have acid reflux or gas.

THE BURP

BURPING MADE SIMPLE

Burping your baby is one of the many tasks parents have to do until baby's digestive system is more mature. Burps are caused by excess gas from the stomach or upper intestine that is released from the mouth. Until babies can handle gas themselves (between the ages of eight and nine months), you will be helping that gas along.

TIPS ON BURPING A BABY

- Always keep a burp cloth between your outfit and baby's mouth to catch any spit-up or drool.

- A gentle pat or rub may get the burp out for most babies, but some need a slightly firmer hand.

- Focus on the left side of baby's back, which is where your little one's stomach is located.

- Fussiness in the middle of a feeding may be because your baby is uncomfortable from swallowing air during feeding. Try burping baby to see if air is released. That may have been what caused your baby to refuse to continue eating.

Daddy Hack

Over the shoulder was my go-to burping method. I found that if I added a little gentle bouncing motion, I was pretty much guaranteed to get a burp.

THE TOP BURPING METHODS

METHOD #1
OVER THE SHOULDER

Your baby's chin should rest on your shoulder as you support baby with one arm across baby's butt. (Basically, baby is sitting on your arm.) With your other hand, gently pat your baby's back while you are sitting or standing.

METHOD #2
SITTING UP

Hold your baby sitting up on your lap. Support the baby's chest and head with one hand by cradling your baby's chin in your palm, but be careful to grip your baby's chin, not baby's throat. Use the other hand to pat your baby's back.

METHOD #3
FACEDOWN LAP

Place baby lying tummy down across your lap with head turned to one side. Steady baby with one hand under baby's body, and with your other hand, gently pat or rub baby's back. NOTE: Not my favorite—I found that with baby lying down, baby tends to spit up more.

WEANING BABY
SAYING GOODBYE TO THE BOTTLE

There are two main ways to lose the bottle: going cold turkey or slowly removing it. No matter which method, there will be some degree of push back. We chose to slowly remove the bottle, until we were only giving a bottle in the morning and night, progressively putting less and less milk in the bottle until our kids just did not want it.

MAKING THE BIG SWITCH

Because your child has grown attached to the bottle, the thought of taking it away can be daunting. The key to a stress-free transition from the bottle to a cup is planning ahead and being consistent.

INTRODUCE WATER IN A SIPPY CUP — 6 MONTHS

REMOVE OR REDUCE BOTTLE USE AT MEALS — 8 MONTHS

BOTTLE 2–3 TIMES A DAY — 11 MONTHS

BOTTLE FREE — 18–24 MONTHS

TIPS FOR DITCHING THE BOTTLE

- **CHOOSE A STRESS-FREE TIME**

  It's wise to begin weaning the bottle when there will be no major disruptions. You would not want to start when on vacation, moving into a new home, etc.

- **INTRODUCE THE CUP EARLY**

  Around six to eight months, start introducing the sippy cup, letting your baby hold and become familiar with it. Help baby take a sip.

- **SUBSTITUTE ONCE A DAY**

  At age nine to eleven months, substitute a sippy cup for a bottle at one daytime feeding. Every week, introduce the cup at another feeding, and slowly decrease the number of bottles your child receives.

- **TAKE IT SLOW**

  Be patient and take your time: it is a gradual process.

- **OUT OF SIGHT, OUT OF MIND**

  As you begin reducing the use of the bottle, it can be helpful to keep the bottles out of sight so your child is not reminded about the missing bottle.

- **PRAISE, PRAISE, PRAISE**

  When a child drinks from a cup, be sure to give lots of praise. Say how impressed you are that the child is drinking just like you.

- **BE CONSISTENT**

  Consistency is key to successfully removing the bottle. Be sure to give your child the cup at feeding times and don't switch back to the bottle.

COW'S MILK AND MILK SUBSTITUTES

It is recommended that a child under the age of one year **NOT** be given cow's milk or milk substitutes in place of formula or breast milk. They do not supply all the appropriate nutrition for baby.

THE MUST-HAVES
INTRODUCING SOLIDS

1 FOOD PROCESSOR | BABY FOOD MAKER

Unless you plan on using store-bought baby food, you will be making your own. This can be quick, easy, and very cost-effective if you have the right equipment. The difference between a processor and food maker is that with a processor you have to cook the food separately, and then puree it, whereas a food maker is an all-in-one device.

8–10 STORAGE JARS

If you are making purees yourself, you will need food storage jars. You should make sure that they are 100 percent BPA- and phthalate-free and both freezer, and dishwasher safe. Many of the baby food makers also come with some jars.

3–4 SPOONS & FORKS

Look for soft-tipped spoons and forks specifically for babies that are gentle on your child's gums and limit portions to tiny spoonfuls. Make sure they are 100 percent BPA- and phthalate-free and dishwasher safe.

3 BABY BOWLS

Choose bowls that are 100 percent BPA- and phthalate-free and dishwasher safe. A big plus is if they are microwavable and they come with lids for storage.

5 PLATES

Choose plates (NO GLASS) that are 100 percent BPA- and phthalate-free and dishwasher safe. It's a plus if they are microwavable.

1 HIGH CHAIR

When shopping for a high chair, look for one that is easy to use and clean (with a removable and machine-washable seat pad). It should have a removable tray, safety-seat straps (with 3- to 5-point harness), and wheels that move easily and lock. It's a plus if it can convert to a chair as baby grows. Consider whether it can store easily, fold up, and slide under the table.

1 POPSICLE MOLD

This is a fun addition to the array of foods your toddler will love. You should make sure that they are BPA- and phthalate-free and dishwasher safe.

2 SNACK CONTAINERS

Instead of handing out one snack at a time, these solve that problem and prevent snacks from spilling everywhere. They are also great for travel. Be sure they are BPA- and phthalate-free and dishwasher safe.

5–10 STORAGE CONTAINERS

As you transition to more solid foods, you may need additional containers for your infant's food. These should be BPA- and phthalate-free and dishwasher safe. Additionally, it's a plus if they are microwave safe, avoiding the need to transfer the food to something else for warming up.

2–3 SIPPY CUPS

Around the same time that your little one is beginning to migrate to solid foods, your child will also be starting to use a sippy cup. The cups should be BPA- and phthalate-free and dishwasher safe.

GET THE RIGHT STUFF!

Go to Simplestbaby.com for recommendations of the smartest baby products and essentials.

SOLID FOOD
MILESTONES | STAGES

SIGNS THAT YOUR BABY IS READY FOR SOLIDS

- Baby can sit up well and hold head straight without support.
- Baby does not automatically spit out solids from the mouth.
- Baby moves his mouth in a chewing motion.
- Baby picks up objects with thumb and forefinger "pincer" grasp.
- Baby is interested in your food, and tries to grab it and put it in baby's own mouth.

FOOD ALLERGIES

If your baby is allergic to a new food, you'll typically see signs of a reaction within a few minutes or hours. Most children with food allergies have mild reactions. If you notice hives, vomiting, or diarrhea, call your baby's doctor for advice as soon as possible.

If you notice wheezing, difficulty breathing, or facial swelling (including of the tongue and lips), your baby may be having a life-threatening reaction called anaphylaxis. **Call 911** or your local emergency number immediately.

QUICK TIP

Recent evidence supports introducing the typical allergenic food to baby even at the age of four to six months. This may help reduce the risk of a child developing allergies to those foods. Consult your doctor before introducing.

TYPICAL ALLERGENIC FOODS
Cow's Milk, Eggs, Fish, Shellfish, Peanuts, Tree Nuts, Wheat, and Soy

SOLIDS & MILK

Breast milk or formula will still provide the majority of your baby's calories and nutrition until baby is one year old. Both provide important vitamins, iron, and protein in a form that's easy to digest. Solid food will eventually replace the nutrients that breast milk or formula provided during the first year.

INTRODUCING SOLID FOODS

1
SOLID FOOD

EVERY

3–5
DAYS

Start with a pureed single-ingredient food with no salt or sugar added. Offer one new food over three to five days before trying another new food. This way you'll be able to tell if baby has any allergic reaction, discomfort, or constipation.

Daddy Hack

Using a soft-tipped plastic spoon to feed your baby can help avoid injuring her gums. They also make great teethers when those teeth start coming in.

4–6 MONTHS

At four to six months, you will potentially start introducing purees. Solids readiness depends on the maturity of baby's digestive system and developmental readiness. Each baby is different and will be ready at different times.

FOODS TO START WITH FOR PUREE

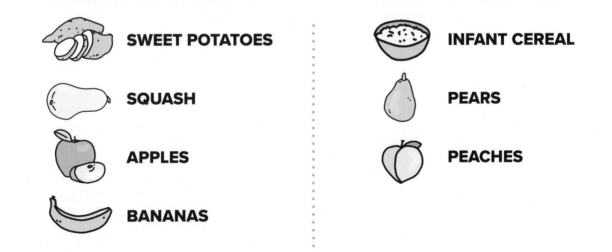

SWEET POTATOES

SQUASH

APPLES

BANANAS

INFANT CEREAL

PEARS

PEACHES

PUREE IDEAS

For quick and simple puree combinations that your little one might like, go to: Simplestbaby.com/pureerecipes

SOLID FOOD
MILESTONES | STAGES

6–8 MONTHS

At six to eight months, you can begin to introduce additional foods that are pureed, strained, or mashed. You will still give breast milk or formula to your baby, but you should begin to introduce drinking from a sippy cup at some of your baby's meals.

6–8 MONTH FOODS

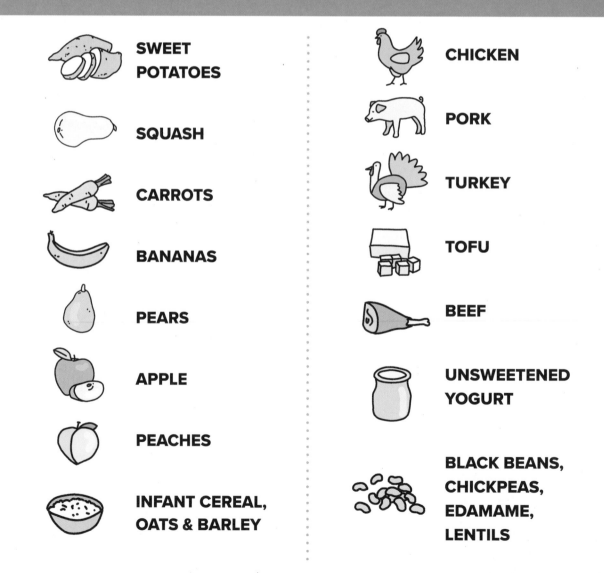

- SWEET POTATOES
- SQUASH
- CARROTS
- BANANAS
- PEARS
- APPLE
- PEACHES
- INFANT CEREAL, OATS & BARLEY

- CHICKEN
- PORK
- TURKEY
- TOFU
- BEEF
- UNSWEETENED YOGURT
- BLACK BEANS, CHICKPEAS, EDAMAME, LENTILS

8–10 MONTHS

At eight to ten months, baby can start eating chunkier soft foods, chopped into fine pieces or mashed. You will begin to introduce additional new foods, and many babies will be eating three "meals" per day.

8–10 MONTH FOODS

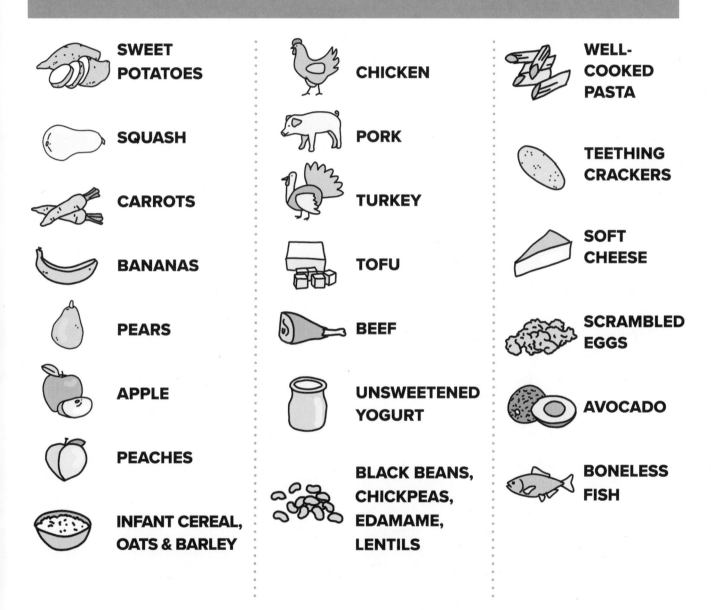

SWEET POTATOES

SQUASH

CARROTS

BANANAS

PEARS

APPLE

PEACHES

INFANT CEREAL, OATS & BARLEY

CHICKEN

PORK

TURKEY

TOFU

BEEF

UNSWEETENED YOGURT

BLACK BEANS, CHICKPEAS, EDAMAME, LENTILS

WELL-COOKED PASTA

TEETHING CRACKERS

SOFT CHEESE

SCRAMBLED EGGS

AVOCADO

BONELESS FISH

PUREE IDEAS

For quick and simple puree combinations that your little one might like, go to: Simplestbaby.com/pureerecipes

SOLID FOOD
MILESTONES | STAGES

1 YEAR

When your little one has reached one year of age, you should make meals a combination of soft foods toddlers can eat with their hands and foods you spoon-feed.

3 meals + 2 snacks per day

The meals should include lots of fruits and vegetables, eggs, meat, and fish.

ORGANIC COW'S MILK

One of the biggest dietary changes occurring when your baby turns one is the introduction of organic whole milk.

The American Academy of Pediatrics suggests children get 16 to 24 ounces of milk a day, since the calcium is necesary for strong bones and teeth. Children under the age of one year should not be given cow's milk.

FOOD WARNINGS:

BEWARE OF SUGAR

As a general rule, one-year-old babies should not eat sweets. You should also be careful about hidden sugars that are found in many products, as excess sugar can cause tooth decay and obesity. Avoid giving toddlers fruit drinks, sodas, or beverages with added color, flavors, and gases.

Daddy Hack

GRAPES: My daughter loves grapes, but there's a high level of risk of kids choking on them. To reduce that risk:
1. Only buy seedless grapes.
2. Always cut the grapes into halves or quarters.
3. Use mesh food pouches that baby can chew on.

BEWARE OF HONEY

Never feed honey to a child under the age of one year old. A baby can get botulism by ingesting spores found in soil, honey, and honey products. These spores grow into bacteria in the bowels and produce harmful neurotoxins in the body.

THE RIGHT SOLID FOOD FOR YOUR ONE-YEAR-OLD

Toddlers can eat most things that you do; however, as their digestive systems are still developing, you will want to stay away from spicy foods. You should still be careful of foods that are choking hazards, such as nuts, grapes, popcorn, and hot dogs.

FEEDING TIP

When feeding baby food from a jar, it is best to put what you will be feeding baby into a separate bowl, so you don't potentially contaminate any leftovers in the jar with bacteria from baby's mouth.

Whoever
says they sleep
like a baby, doesn't
have one.

SWEET DREAMS, PLEASE!

What to know for baby (and you) to sleep

SLEEPING
TYPICAL MILESTONES

	NEWBORN 1 MONTH	2–3 MONTHS
SLEEP PER 24 HOURS	• About **18–20 hours**	• About **16–17 hours**
NIGHT SLEEP	• **Wake every two to three hours** to feed baby • You hardly sleep	• You sleep **intermittently** during the night
DAY SLEEP	• **Same as above** Wake baby up every two to three hours for feeding	• About **three to four (or even more) naps a day**
TECHNIQUE	**SWADDLE**	**SWADDLE**

Getting your baby to sleep through the night is one of the most important tasks of a parent, it can also be one of the hardest and most frustrating. The timeline below outlines the general age for accomplishing these milestones. It is worth noting that every baby is different, and some flexibility is required, especially for premature babies or babies with medical conditions.

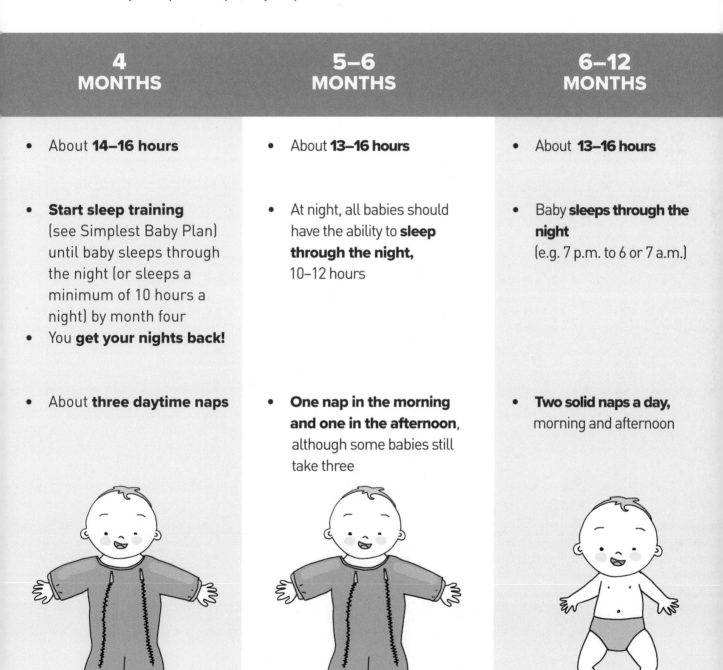

4 MONTHS	5–6 MONTHS	6–12 MONTHS
• About **14–16 hours**	• About **13–16 hours**	• About **13–16 hours**
• **Start sleep training** (see Simplest Baby Plan) until baby sleeps through the night (or sleeps a minimum of 10 hours a night) by month four • You **get your nights back!**	• At night, all babies should have the ability to **sleep through the night,** 10–12 hours	• Baby **sleeps through the night** (e.g. 7 p.m. to 6 or 7 a.m.)
• About **three daytime naps**	• **One nap in the morning and one in the afternoon**, although some babies still take three	• **Two solid naps a day,** morning and afternoon
SWADDLE ALTERNATIVE	**SWADDLE ALTERNATIVE**	**I'M FREE**

THE MUST-HAVES
WHAT YOU NEED FOR THE NIGHT

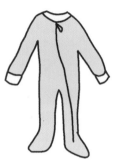

4–5 PAJAMAS

Be economical by purchasing the minimum number of pajamas as your baby will outgrow them fast! Avoid hoods or loose-fitting pj's that could pose a suffocation or fire hazard. Consider lighter-weight pajamas for summer and heavier during the winter, depending on the temperature of your home.

OVERNIGHT DIAPERS

Typically more absorbent than the daytime variety, they are designed to keep baby dry all night long to avoid the mess of leaky diapers.

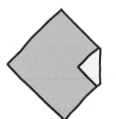

3 SWADDLES OR SWADDLE ALTERNATIVES

A blanket designed to be wrapped in a specific manner in order to help baby sleep better by comforting and keeping baby warm and secure. Look for ones made of soft pure cotton or muslin.

2 SLEEP SUITS | SACKS

Patented swaddle transition products designed for back sleeping in a crib. Provides a cozy, secure feeling and helps reduce baby's startle reflexes to aid in sleeping.

1 WHITE-NOISE MACHINE

This device creates calming white noises. Look for ones that have multiple sound settings and options. They encourage babies to stop crying, fall asleep faster, and stay asleep longer.

2–3 PACIFIERS

Made from silicone or latex that is BPA-free. Pacifier nipples come in one of two varieties: a standard round nipple and an orthodontic shape. Both work well. Pacifiers come in several sizes.

1 BABY MONITOR

Choose a video or wireless monitor that can be recharged or plugged in. Night vision guarantees a clearer image when the lights are low or off. It should have the ability to zoom in, and the lens should be able to turn so when the baby moves it can follow. It should also have the ability to monitor the room temperature.

GET THE RIGHT STUFF!
Go to Simplestbaby.com for recommendations of the smartest baby products and essentials.

SAFE SLEEPING
SIDS PREVENTION

Sudden infant death syndrome (SIDS) is the unexplained death of a seemingly healthy baby while he or she sleeps. Things to know about putting your baby to sleep safely and lowering the risk of SIDS.

BACK SLEEPING IS THE SAFEST

To reduce the risk of sudden infant death syndrome, the safest sleep position is **ALWAYS** on their backs.

BABY RISK FACTORS

- **Gender:** Boys are slightly more likely to die of SIDS

- **Age:** Infants who are between the second and fourth months of age

- **Being premature:** Babies born early or who have a low birth weight

- **Race:** Nonwhite infants are at a higher risk of SIDS

- **Family history:** Babies whose siblings or cousins died of SIDS

- **Secondhand smoke:** Babies in a home with a smoker

PARENTAL RISK FACTORS

- Moms younger than 20

- Poor prenatal care

- Smoking tobacco around baby

- Drug or alcohol use

Tips to reduce the risk of SIDS

To prevent suffocation risk, **DON'T USE A BUMPER,** unless it is breathable mesh.

Make sure the crib **MATTRESS IS FIRM.**

Always put baby to sleep on her back, **NEVER ON HER STOMACH OR SIDE.**

NO SMOKING around the baby.

Make sure your baby is **UP TO DATE WITH VACCINES.**

KEEP PLUSH TOYS AND BLANKETS OUT OF THE CRIB. Make sure the sheet is tightly fitted to prevent risk of suffocation.

Prevent baby from overheating. Keep room temperature between **68°F–72°F.**

GOOD NIGHT
YOU & BABY GET A GOOD NIGHT'S SLEEP

Daddy Hack

An inexpensive way to create your own white-noise device is by recording a vacuum, TV or radio static, or a washing machine on your phone. You can also use one of the various music apps to find white noise.

SIMPLE STEPS TO HELP BABY SLEEP

ESTABLISH A BEDTIME ROUTINE

Have a set time for going to bed and a consistent 15- to 30-minute bedtime routine. The routine can be as simple as giving baby a bath, putting on a nighttime diaper and pajamas, and then dimming the lights, reading a book, and giving a bottle.

SWADDLE YOUR BABY

Swaddling is a method of wrapping a baby in a blanket that keeps the baby's arms and legs tucked close to her body, so they stay in place and don't wake her up. Swaddling is thought to be soothing to babies as it gives them a feeling of security, like in the womb.

LIMIT EYE CONTACT

Eye contact has been proven to be stimulating to babies, so during night feedings and changes and just before going to bed, you should limit prolonged eye contact.

CONTROL THE ROOM TEMPERATURE

Keeping your baby's room between the temperatures of **68°F and 72°F** has been shown to help babies sleep better. Avoid letting the room get too hot, as it has been found to be a potential factor in causing SIDS.

KEEP IT DARK AND USE A DIMMER

Newborns don't have a fully functioning circadian rhythm yet. During night feedings and diaper changes, keep it dark or use light on low dimmers. This way, you will help establish your baby's circadian rhythm.

USE A WHITE-NOISE MACHINE

Infants find rhythmic sounds comforting, especially those that are similar to what they heard in the womb. Do not turn up the volume too high to protect against any hearing damage.

CUT THE CAFFEINE

If you are breastfeeding, keep in mind that the caffeine you drink will affect your baby's sleep.

PRACTICE SOFT BABY MASSAGE

Some parents have found giving their baby a 15-minute gentle massage at bedtime helps baby fall asleep more quickly and wake less during the night.

OFFER ONE LAST FEEDING

Whether breastfeeding or bottle feeding, one last feeding before bed will help baby sleep longer.

Daddy Hack

ISSUE: At four months of age baby is waking an hour or two early. **TIP:** Add fine baby oatmeal to baby's last bottle so baby stays full longer. You will need to get a larger nipple size as even fine oatmeal will clog smaller sizes.

TRADITIONAL SWADDLE
HELPING YOU & BABY SLEEP BETTER

0–4 MONTHS

WHAT IS IT?

Swaddling is the snug wrapping of an infant in a square-shaped blanket that restricts the movement of baby's arms and legs. It creates the familiar soothing feeling a baby experienced in the womb. It can also help a baby fall asleep more quickly and stay asleep longer. Swaddling is only for back sleeping.

Although most babies sleep better when swaddled, some don't. If this is the case for your baby, then you might try one of the other swaddle alternatives or skip it altogether.

HOW TO SWADDLE STEP-BY-STEP

1 On a flat surface, arrange the blanket in a diamond shape, folding the top corner down slightly. Place baby face up on the blanket so that the shoulders are aligned with the straight top.

2 Bring baby's right arm down to his side and gently hold it there while you bring the same side of the blanket across the body, tucking it under the left side of baby's body.

WARNING: SWADDLE CAUTIONS

TOO LOOSE

Swaddles that are too loose could become unwrapped during sleep and cover your baby's face, creating the potential for suffocation and SIDS.

TOO TIGHT

Swaddles that are too snug around your baby's hips could damage them.

TOO HOT

Swaddling can increase the chance your baby will overheat, so avoid letting your baby get too hot. If you notice sweating, damp hair, flushed cheeks, heat rash, or rapid breathing, make sure room temp is 68°F to 72°F max and that baby is dressed only in a diaper when swaddled.

WHEN TO STOP SWADDLING

Once baby begins to roll over, you should **STOP** swaddling.

3 Bring the bottom corner of the blanket up, covering the legs, and tuck it under the first fold, under baby's left shoulder. The legs should still be able to move.

4 Take the left arm and lay it straight to the baby's side. Bring the last corner snugly across the body, wrapping it behind baby's back and tucking the end inside the blanket in back.

EASIER WAY TO SWADDLE
NEW SWADDLING BLANKETS & ALTERNATIVES

WHAT'S NEW

Today's new generation of swaddles come in a wide range of styles and designs. They have a variety of closures, pockets, and flaps built in that make swaddling baby more convenient and far easier.

- **Swaddle Blanket Updates**

  These new swaddle blankets come with sewn-in pockets for legs and flaps which make swaddling much simpler.

- **Swaddle Sacks**

  These are sleep sacks (wearable blankets) that also have special closures ranging from Velcro to buttons to snaps.

- **Stretchy Pods**

  These are pods made of soft stretchy spandex cotton blends that you simply zip your baby into.

WHEN TO STOP SWADDDLING

Once baby begins to roll over or shows signs that she might, you should stop swaddling completely. This can happen at around 14 weeks of age (unless baby begins to roll over sooner). When this happens, it's time to transition to a sleep suit or sleep sack.

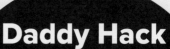

Daddy Hack

Like all things baby, not everything works for all babies and you will need to test out what works best for you. Our personal favorite was the Miracle Blanket®: we found it simple and easy to use with both our children.

WHAT'S NEXT
TRANSITIONING OUT OF THE SWADDLE

3–4 MONTHS

OK, you have stopped using the swaddle, but your baby still needs more time to develop stronger neck, arm, and leg muscles. This is where the transition sleep products come in. They allow your baby to sleep safely while providing the additional time that your baby may need to continue developing.

WHAT ARE TRANSITION SLEEP PRODUCTS?

These products help babies transition from a swaddle to sleeping on their own more safely. They allow babies time to strengthen their back, neck, core, arms, and legs so that they are strong enough to roll over on their own.

- **Sleep Suits**

    These sleep outfits provide warmth and support like a swaddle but with the added freedom to move arms and legs. These suits are usually slightly padded for weight to prevent baby from rolling over. They also help reduce baby twitches and startle movements from waking them.

- **Sleep Sacks**

    Similar to a sleeping bag, but these have arm holes and are slightly padded for weight to prevent baby from rolling over.

TIPS FOR USING A SLEEP SUIT

- Sleep suits are specifically designed for back sleeping ONLY.

- Sleep suits are designed to be used in an empty crib.

- Not recommended for co-sleeping or for use with any sleep positioners.

- Room temperature should be at the appropriate level.

- Stop using a sleep suit if baby is able to roll over while wearing it or shows signs that she might!

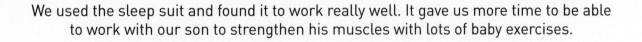

SLEEPING TEMPERATURE

68°F to 72°F

The recommended room temperature for a baby to sleep in both winter and summer.

We used the sleep suit and found it to work really well. It gave us more time to be able to work with our son to strengthen his muscles with lots of baby exercises.

CRYING
TEACHING BABY TO SELF SOOTHE

When baby cries, you will be picking him up to check on and comfort. At around three months, you will need to start managing this urge. Babies are learning machines and learn quickly how to manipulate caregivers. They can learn that crying gets them picked up and comforted on demand. It may seem like a harmless thing to always pick up and comfort baby, but over time, this can become a real problem.

You run the risk of not being able to put baby down without prolonged crying even though there is nothing wrong. You are now on the path to never sleeping again. Before you get to this point, when baby starts crying, you need to take a moment and wait. The general rule is when you put baby down and baby starts to cry, you let him, assuming you have cleared the following checklist below:

BABY-CRYING CHECKLIST

✓ Has baby been fed?

✓ Has baby been burped?

✓ Does baby have a clean diaper?

✓ Does baby have gas?

✓ Does baby have a fever?

✓ Is baby having teething pain?

HOW IT WORKS

After checking off the baby-crying checklist, it's time to pause. Let the baby cry for 15-20 minutes. If the crying persists, check on the baby, as it's likely that something is wrong, the baby may have pooped, need to burp, or have gas. Starting this technique early and being consistent is very important. During the first month, you will **NOT** use this technique, as baby will be up and down fairly regularly for feeding. It's in months two and three that you can begin using this technique.

PAUSE FOR
15–20
MINUTES

SLEEP TRAINING
GET YOUR SLEEP BACK

QUICK TIP

Before beginning to teach baby to fall asleep on her own, you should have her on a regular schedule, putting her to bed at a consistent time each night.

The thought that you will never sleep again is one that every parent has. And you will find that sleep is one of the most impacted areas of new parents' life.

WHAT IS SLEEP TRAINING?

Sleep training teaches babies to fall asleep and stay asleep all night without waking to feed, be soothed, or be changed. For some lucky parents, this happens easily, but for most, it's more challenging. Sleep training is intended to teach babies who wake up during the night to soothe themselves back to sleep.

NOTE: Various sleep training methods are controversial, and every parent will need to determine which, if any, are right for their baby.

WHEN TO START

For a healthy baby, sleep training potentially can start at four to five months, depending on the weight of the baby.

WHEN TO BEGIN SLEEP TRAINING

12–13 lbs. | 4–5 months old

This is when babies reach a point that they can self soothe and sleep through the night without needing to feed.

IS BABY READY?

If your child is gaining weight slowly or is a preemie, your baby may not be ready to begin dropping nighttime feedings and may need a sleep-training schedule adapted to his specific needs. Infants should have no medical concerns and have a healthy growth curve approved by your pediatrician to begin sleep training.

SLEEP-TRAINING METHODS

EXTINCTION | CRY IT OUT (CIO)

This technique involves putting your baby to bed and letting baby cry until he falls asleep without any comfort or help from you.

You've put your baby to bed with a full tummy and in a safe environment, and are not to return until it's time for baby to get up the next morning or until baby needs to eat next.

FERBER METHOD

The Ferber Method is an extinction technique. It involves letting baby cry a set period of time before soothing. Progressively over several nights, you increase the length of time before you check on baby; eventually, baby will learn to self soothe.

CHAIR METHOD

You begin by sitting in a chair next to baby's crib, without picking baby up, until baby falls asleep. If baby cries, you do not pick him up and soothe. Each night, you move the chair farther away until you're eventually out of the room altogether.

BEDTIME FADING METHOD

When baby starts to show signs of being sleepy, put baby to bed. Ideally baby will fall asleep, but if he starts crying a lot, take baby out of the crib. Soothe him for a set amount of time (half an hour) and then try again. After a few nights of putting baby down at that time, move bedtime back in 15-minute increments, repeating until you reach the desired bedtime.

PICK UP, PUT DOWN METHOD

Put the baby to bed and if baby cries, you wait a few minutes to see if baby goes back to sleep by himself. If not, you pick baby up and, once soothed, put baby back to bed. Repeat these steps until your baby falls asleep. This can be a long process and requires lots of patience.

SLEEP REGRESSION

Wait a minute, we're moving in the wrong direction.

Everything seems to be going well with baby sleeping but then baby's sleep pattern starts to shift, creating problems. As babies develop, it is normal to have setbacks; these are temporary and can be caused by baby's natural growth and development, baby teething, discomfort, etc.

SIMPLEST BABY SLEEP SCHEDULING
AN ALTERNATIVE TO SLEEP TRAINING

Sleep training can be a difficult and frustrating process for lots of parents. There is an alternative: Simplest Baby Sleep Scheduling.

Having baby on a schedule makes life so much easier because you have set times for all baby activities. It also makes it easier for others to step in and help out, as they have a schedule to follow for eating, playing, sleeping, etc.

We used this method for our children, and one slept through the night at three months, the other at four months. It requires that you strictly and consistently follow the day and night schedules. For some parents this may be too rigid, but I swear by it.

WHAT IS IT?

Sleep scheduling means following a specific day and night schedule for baby; you track activities, especially feedings, so that you can slowly drop out nighttime feedings until baby is sleeping through the night without waking to feed.

What happens during the day affects what happens during the night.

1 RAMP UP VOLUME OF FOOD DURING THE DAY

It is important that you follow the daytime schedules for feeding, sleeping, playing, and bathing. The combination of these activities during the day will help your baby learn to sleep through the night and help your baby achieve other developmental milestones. The schedule will help you track feeding quantities as you steadily increase the amount of food baby eats during the day.

2 REDUCE THE NUMBER OF FEEDINGS AT NIGHT

As you increase the amount of milk your baby is consuming during the day, you will progressively reduce the number of feedings needed at night, gradually dropping all nighttime feedings.

Adding **1 OZ.** during the day = **1 HOUR** extra sleep at night

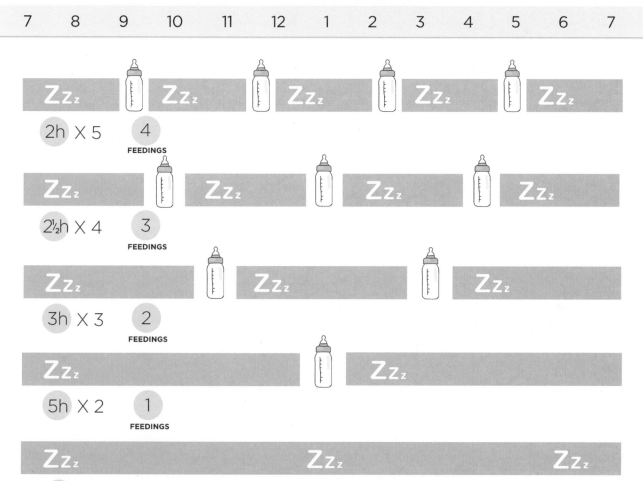

3 EXTEND SLEEP PERIODS

As baby is able to sleep longer without waking up hungry, you will continue to reduce the number of feedings at night while letting the sleep period continue to extend.

4 SLEEPING THROUGH THE NIGHT

CO-SLEEPING
ALL TOGETHER NOW

Co-sleeping essentially means sleeping in close proximity to your child.

WHAT IS IT?

Co-sleeping is the practice of baby sleeping close to one or both parents in baby's own bed or in the same bed instead of in a separate room.

There are several variations of co-sleeping:

1. Sidecar arrangement:

A crib is placed against one side of the parents' bed. The side of the crib against the parents' bed is lowered or removed so that the parent has easy access to the baby.

2. Different beds in the same room:

Baby's bassinet or crib is in the same room as the parents—close enough that the parents can easily reach it.

3. Sleeping with parent as needed:

Baby has her own bedroom but is brought to the parents' bed as needed.

4. Bed sharing/family bed:

Parent(s) sleep in the same bed with the baby.

IS BED SHARING SAFE? NO

Sleeping in the same bed with your baby can be dangerous. You increase the risk of SIDS when a baby is not sleeping on a flat surface with a tight, fitted sheet.

If you are a parent who is a deep sleeper, you run the risk of rolling over on the baby and suffocating her. There is also the possibility baby will fall out of the bed.

CO-SLEEPING & SIDS

A baby sleeping in your room actually reduces the risk of SIDS. The AAP recommends that babies sleep in the same room (but not in the same bed) as the parents for a minimum of six months and up to a year, if you can.

PERSONAL PREFERENCE

Whether you choose to co-sleep or not is a personal preference and depends on your family's unique needs.

Oops, I did it
again and again
and again.

UNDERSTANDING POOP

You may have dealt with a lot of shit in your life; now you get to deal with a lot more—literally. This section is designed to help you understand and deal with your baby's poop.

THE MUST-HAVES
WHAT YOU NEED TO DEAL WITH POOP

1 CHANGING PAD

Look for one that is waterproof with contoured sides and easily wipes clean. It should have adjustable safety straps to buckle in baby and anchoring straps to hold it to whatever surface it is on.

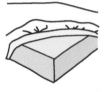

2 CHANGING PAD COVERS

You will want an absorbent, comfortable, waterproof cover that is easy to clean and will hold up to frequent washing.

1 DIAPER PAIL

Choose a waterproof, tall pail with good capacity that has an odor-control device. Look for a pail that opens by using a foot pedal. Consider a pail with a childproof lock or one that can have a lock added.

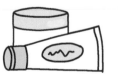

1 DIAPER RASH CREAM

Creams should contain a high percentage of zinc oxide. These creams are generally effective for treating mild-to-moderate irritations, but may not work for severe rashes. An option for more severe cases of diaper rash is butt paste.

WIPES

Use biodegradable, unscented, hypoallergenic, paraben- and fragrance-free wipes.

HAND SANITIZER

Pick one that contains 60 percent ethyl alcohol or 70 percent isopropyl alcohol, with few other ingredients.

GET THE RIGHT STUFF!
Go to Simplestbaby.com for recommendations of the smartest baby products and essentials.

CHANGING STATION
PUTTING IT TOGETHER

Here is what you will need for the ideal changing station. If you have a two-story home, you might consider having one upstairs for nighttime and one downstairs for daytime changes.

HAND SANITIZER

WIPES

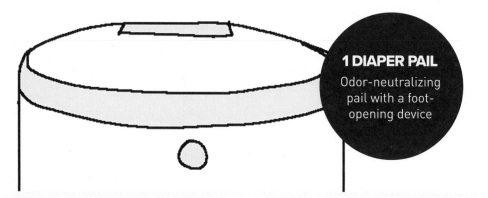

1 DIAPER PAIL
Odor-neutralizing pail with a foot-opening device

GET THE RIGHT STUFF!
Go to Simplestbaby.com for recommendations of the smartest baby products and essentials.

CHANGING PAD & CHANGING PAD COVERS

Daddy Hack

Using a large-size doggy pee pad as a cover for the foam changing pad is a Daddy hack to catch any stray pee, poo, or spit-up that is bound to happen and cuts down on washing.

1 FIRST AID & PERSONAL CARE KIT

A changing station is the perfect place to take care of other basic baby stuff, like nail clipping, taking temperatures, or giving medicine.

VASELINE
INFANT Q-TIPS
COTTON BALLS
STERILE GAUZE
1 BABY LOTION

DIAPERS

Lots and lots of daytime and nighttime diapers that are removed from the packaging and nicely stacked so they are ready to use.

DIAPER RASH CREAM

NOSE-CLEANING DEVICE

DIAPERS
WHAT YOU NEED TO KNOW

One of the first decisions you will need to make is whether to use disposable or cloth diapers.

DISPOSABLE DIAPERS

Standard disposable diapers are undeniably more convenient but rather expensive and not environmentally friendly. You can choose an "eco-friendly" disposable diaper, but those are even more expensive. No single-use diaper is biodegradable. Disposable diapers generally come in two types.

1. DAYTIME DIAPERS

A nonwoven fabric diaper with an absorbent chemical pad sandwiched between two sheets. The pad is designed to absorb and retain moisture from pee and poop, keeping the baby dry. Once soiled, they are thrown in the trash.

2. OVERNIGHT DIAPERS

Similar to the daytime diapers but designed with an even more absorbent core to keep your baby dry for up to 12 hours. They are a bit more expensive than daytime diapers.

CLOTH DIAPERS

Cloth diapers are better for the environment and can be less expensive than disposables, especially if you wash them yourself. If you are not interested in doing the washing, there are diaper services that pick up dirty diapers and deliver clean ones.

The initial cost seems high, but the saving comes as you continue to reuse them. Some companies have starter kits of cloth diapers that come with a variety of accessories like cloth-pad inserts, waterproof covers to lock in moisture, and flushable liners.

TYPES OF CLOTH DIAPERS

FLATS

These are the old-fashioned kind: a simple, large, flat square of fabric that you wrap and pin around your baby. They require a waterproof diaper cover.

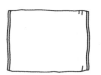

PREFOLDS

Similar to flats, this is a rectangle-shaped fabric with extra-absorbent padding in the center. They require a waterproof diaper cover.

FITTED

These are made from absorbent fabric that has fitted elastic for the legs and waist. Similar to disposable diapers in that they have an hourglass shape, they don't require folding. They usually have their own snap or Velcro closure. They require a waterproof diaper cover.

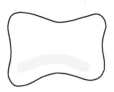

CONTOUR

These diapers are shaped to fit your baby, so you do not need to do any folding. These do not have their own closures.

POCKET

These are made with a waterproof shell with a pocket on the inside, in which an absorbent insert is placed. No outer diaper cover needed; they come with snaps or Velcro closures.

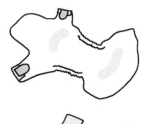

ALL-IN-ONE

This diaper is made in specific sizes and is like a disposable in shape. No outer diaper cover required. There is no inserting or attaching a pad, just flush the poop and the whole thing goes in the wash. Everything is one piece.

HYBRID | ALL-IN-TWO

This diaper uses an insert that is either cloth or disposable that lays inside the outer diaper. It can be used with a biodegradable, disposable, or washable insert. These also come in various sizes.

CHANGING DIAPERS

You should check your baby's diaper before and after every nap. Never let your baby stay in a dirty diaper for too long as this causes diaper rash.

Most diapers today have a wet stripe to indicate that it's time for a change. You may need to pull open the leg hole of the diaper to check if there is a little surprise for you. Most of the time, you will know that a change is needed as the diaper will be heavy, the pee stripe will have changed color, or your nose will tell you.

1 Lay baby on his back. Remove any clothing that prevents access to the diaper. With one hand, lift the baby's legs off the table, holding them by the ankles. Place a clean diaper under the dirty one, in case baby has an accident mid-change.

2 Unfasten side tabs, laying the dirty diaper on top of the clean one. Use wipes to clean the baby and deposit dirty wipes in the dirty diaper. When finished cleaning off the poop, remove and set the dirty diaper aside. If the diaper is just full of pee, you can remove it immediately.

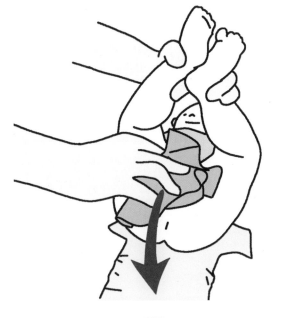

3 When changing boys it's a wise idea to place a wipe over his crotch or you might get a surprise shower. When wiping either poop or pee from female genitals you should wipe from front to back to prevent a urinary tract infection. For boys, wipe in any direction to clean them.

4 If baby's bottom is red or inflamed, soothe it with diaper rash ointment. Bring the front part of the diaper up between baby's legs and fasten the tabs on the side to secure the diaper. If you can't easily fit two fingers between the diaper and your baby, it's too tight.

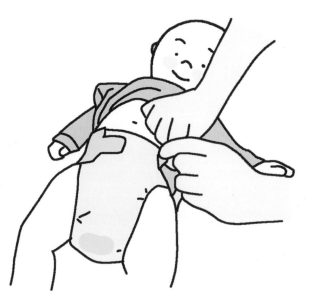

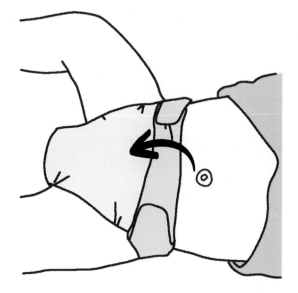

UMBILICAL CORD CARE

For newborns, you will want to fold the top of the diaper down so that it does not cover the umbilical cord, as it can irritate the cord stump and prevent it from drying out.

CIRCUMCISED PENIS CARE

Gently wipe away any bits of poop from the area; it's important to keep this area clean. Apply petroleum jelly or antibiotic ointment after every diaper change for the first several days.

KNOW YOUR SHIT

WHAT YOU NEED TO KNOW

Getting to know your baby's shit is something you probably never thought you would need to do. Well, you actually can tell a lot about babies from what is inside their diapers.

The frequency, color, and consistency of poop will vary by child and what she eats. Some babies go several times a day, and others go every other day.

Normal poop color can be yellow, brown, and even green. If you're ever concerned about your baby's bowel movements, consult your pediatrician for advice. You should also take your baby to the pediatrician if your baby has diarrhea accompanied by a fever.

POOP #1

Your baby's very first poop will not smell bad and will look black and tarry. This is known as meconium, and it's made up of amniotic fluid, mucus, skin cells, and other things ingested while your baby was in utero. This typically lasts only for a couple of days. Most babies have their first poop within 24 hours.

BREASTFED BABY POOP

Around day three to five, a baby's bowel movements turn to a Dijon mustard yellow color with a pasty consistency. It is a bit runny until she gets to solid foods.

FORMULA-FED BABY POOP

Normal formula-fed baby poop is typically a shade of yellow/brown (tan). Formula-fed baby poop is stronger smelling than breastfed baby poop.

RUNNY POOP

Baby diarrhea will be very runny in consistency and can be green, yellow, or brown in color. Mucus and runny poop can indicate an infection or food allergy or sensitivity.

HARD, PELLET-LIKE POOP

If your baby is passing hard poop, more like an adult, that comes out in larger-size, rabbit-like pellets, your baby might be constipated. This can happen if the food baby is getting is too heavy or difficult for the baby to digest, or if baby is dehydrated.

RED POOP

This can be a sign of blood in the poop. Blood found in the stool could be a sign of a milk-protein allergy, while red blood in diarrhea could mean your baby has a bacterial infection. Contact your pediatrician.

BLACK POOP

Black is a sign of digested blood in the gastrointestinal (GI) tract; you should contact your pediatrician.

WHITE POOP

Stools the color of clay can be a sign of a liver-related issue, and you should contact your pediatrician.

TODDLER POOP

When you start to introduce solid foods, you will see a shift in the poop's color depending on what your baby ate. Don't be surprised if you see some undigested pieces of peas or carrots, for example.

DIAPER RASH

It's unavoidable: at some point, your little one will have a diaper rash, and more than likely, several times.

QUICK TIP
For cloth diapers, only use recommended amount of detergents and run an extra rinse cycle to remove traces of detergent. Avoid using fabric softeners and dryer sheets as even these can irritate skin.

WHAT IS IT?

Diaper rash is a common skin inflammation that appears as reddish splotches on your baby's buttocks, thighs, and genitals. In severe cases, the skin can develop lesions or small blisters, and your baby might experience a fever.

CAUSES:

- Being in a wet or dirty diaper too long

- Sleeping in poopy diapers

- Skin rubbing against the diaper

- Having a yeast infection

- Having diarrhea

- Taking antibiotics

- Having a bacterial infection

- Having an allergic reaction to diapers or wet wipes

- Introducing a new food or solid foods in the diet of baby can change the consistency of a baby's poop

- Wearing diapers too tightly

TIPS FOR TREATING

- Treat at the first signs of a rash or redness.

- Check and change the diaper often. As soon as it becomes soiled, change the diaper.

- The skin will be very, very sensitive, so when removing poop off your baby's skin, use a mild cleanser or gentle wipe.

- Try not to rub; instead, gently pat the area clean and dry.

- Use wipes that are fragrance-free and alcohol-free, or use a clean, soft washcloth.

- Let the area completely dry before putting on a new diaper.

- At every diaper change, generously apply diaper rash cream or ointments containing zinc oxide or petroleum, which help to soothe skin and protect it from moisture.

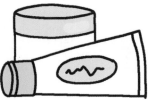

TIPS FOR TREATING BAD CASES

- Use a squirt bottle to wash the area, without rubbing the inflamed skin.

- Air things out a bit before putting the diaper back on. This will help the area heal faster. It might be wise to cover the area where the baby is laying to avoid messy accidents.

WHEN TO CALL THE DOCTOR

- The rash does not go away but gets worse after several days, even after treatment.

- Your baby has a fever or seems sluggish.

- You see yellow pus or discharge from bumps.

- You notice red rash with white scales and lesions, small red pimples outside of the diaper area, or redness in the folds of the baby's skin.

The information provided is not a substitute for professional medical advice, diagnosis, or treatment. Always consult your pediatrician or health-care provider to ensure that a treatment is right for you and your child.

Splish splash,
it's time to take
a bath.

BATHING

Your baby's bath is a big milestone, not to mention a wonderful time for both of you. This section tells you everything you need to know about how, when, and where to bathe your baby.

BATHING
THE MILESTONES

NEWBORN

DESCRIPTION

During the first couple of weeks to a month, you will be giving your baby sponge baths exclusively.

METHOD

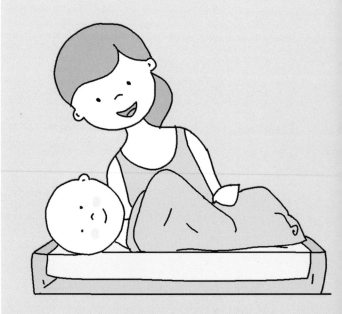

SPONGE BATHING

WARNING:
NEVER LEAVE BABY ALONE IN THE TUB—EVEN AN INCH OF WATER CAN BE DEADLY.

1 MONTH

6+ MONTHS

Once your baby's umbilical cord has dried up and fallen off, and junior's circumcision has healed up, you can graduate to an infant tub.

At around this time, baby is gaining strength; once babies are strong enough to sit up on their own, you can begin having bath time in the tub.

INFANT TUB BATHING

BATHTUB BATHING

THE MUST-HAVES
FOR NEWBORN BATHING

NB
NEWBORN

3 WASHCLOTHS

A regular washcloth will work, but for newborns, the baby washcloths do tend to be softer, smaller, and thinner.

1 BABY SHAMPOO & 1 BABY CLEANSING GEL

Choose soaps that are safe and effective cleansers. They should be tear-free and made from natural ingredients that are hypoallergenic, paraben-free, phthalate-free, phenoxyethanol-free, and fragrance-free.

1 PLASTIC CUP

A plastic cup to pour water over the baby while in the bath is needed. You could use a regular plastic cup or get one that is specifically made with tiny holes in the side so water pours out gently on baby.

1 BOWL OR BASIN

You can use any medium-size bowl you have for this. It is used to hold the warm water during the sponge bath.

2 BATH TOWELS

Keep multiple towels handy in case of big splashes. A towel with a hood is preferred, especially for newborns. Wet babies lose heat fast, and mostly through their heads, so keep your little one bundled up after the bath.

COTTON SWABS | STERILE PADS

Clean cotton swabs or sterile pads for treating the umbilical cord and, if applicable, a circumcised penis.

1 VASELINE

This gel-like cream is made of waxy petroleum. It is used to protect minor cuts and burns, soften skin, minimize friction, and moisturize dry, cracked skin.

1 INFANT BATHTUB

A standalone miniature tub for washing baby before she can sit up by herself in the tub.

BATH FAUCET COVER

A rubber or fabric device that fits over the bath tub faucet to protect little ones from hurting themselves by accidentally bumping into the faucet.

BATH SUPPORT DEVICE

A device used to support baby while being bathed in the bathtub.

GET THE RIGHT STUFF!

Go to Simplestbaby.com for recommendations of the smartest baby products and essentials.

NEWBORN SPONGE BATH

Baby's first bath can be nerve-racking for new parents. Newborn babies are so fragile and seem so delicate that it can be scary thinking you might hurt them. No worries: we have outlined what you need and every step.

BABY'S FIRST BATH

The first bath will be a sponge bath. Pick a warm room with a flat surface, like a bathroom or kitchen counter, a changing table, or a bed. Cover the surface with a thick towel. Make sure the room temperature is at least 75 degrees Fahrenheit because babies chill easily.

For newborns, a sponge bath one, two, three times a week should be sufficient. Keep in mind that you shouldn't fully immerse baby in water until the umbilical cord falls off. For circumcised baby boys, sponge baths should continue until the penis is healed.

WHAT YOU NEED

- A flat surface or curved changing pad
- 2 towels
- 1 washcloth
- 1 plastic bowl
- Warm water
- Clean diaper
- Baby clothing
- Infant soap | shampoo
- 1 plastic cup

WARNING

Water temperature should be between **95°F** and **100°F** MAXIMUM.

1 STEP

Spread two towels over a flat surface or changing pad. Then, undress baby while she is lying on her back. Leave the diaper on (wash that area last). Wrap baby in one of the towels.

2 STEP

With a bowl of warm water and a small amount of soap, dampen the washcloth and cleanse one area at a time. Start with the face, around the baby's eyes, nose, ears, and chin. Then rewet the cloth and move to the neck, arms, legs, and between fingers and toes. Be sure to clean all the creases under the arms, behind the ears, and around the neck, while exposing only those areas that are being washed.

3 STEP

Now it's time to remove the diaper and wash baby's belly, bottom, and genitals. Pat dry all areas after you clean them. Avoid getting the umbilical cord wet.

4 STEP

The hair comes toward the end of the bath, so baby doesn't get cold. You can use a tiny bit of baby shampoo. Cradle the baby's head in your hand over the bowl of warm water. Use a cup to pour water over the hair area of the head, only to rinse. Then position baby's back on the flat surface and dry baby's hair.

5 STEP

When washing girls' genitalia, always wipe from front to back. If your baby boy is uncircumcised, leave the foreskin alone. If circumcised, don't wash the head of the penis until it's healed. Gently pat baby dry. Bath time is over, and your fresh little baby is ready for a clean diaper and clothes!

THE MUST-HAVES
FOR INFANT TUB BATHING

ADDING MORE PRODUCTS

As your baby grows, your bathing method will change. You will use all the items you obtained to give your child a sponge bath, but you will be adding a few new ones as your baby graduates to a bath in an infant tub and then the bathtub.

1 MONTH

INFANT TUB BATHING

Now that the baby's umbilical cord has dried up and fallen off, or junior's circumcision has healed, you can graduate to an infant tub.

1 BABY INFANT TUB

This is a contoured, hard, plastic tub that allows the infant to sit in a slightly upright position, with removable mesh or a fabric sling to keep baby in place. Having a drain plug for easy emptying helps. Smooth edges and an overhanging rim make it easier to pick up and ensure that your baby's skin won't get scratched. A tub that has a nonskid surface to keep your baby in place during bath time is helpful.

1 BABY MOISTURIZING LOTION

A hypoallergenic, fragrance-free baby lotion for possible pre-bedtime baby massage.

BATTHUB BATHING

Now that your baby has gained enough muscular strength to sit up by himself, without your support, you can begin bathing your baby in the bathtub. Here are some additional items you will need.

1 BATHTUB FAUCET COVER

The bathtub spout cover is a thick and soft device that covers the faucet, protecting children from bruising and bumping themselves on the spout when taking a bath.

1 NONSLIP BATHTUB MAT

Get a skid-resistant, BPA-free, latex-free, and phthalate-free mat for the interior of the tub to prevent baby from slipping while bathing.

OVERNIGHT DIAPERS

As your baby is beginning to sleep longer through the night, having overnight diapers are very handy. These are more absorbent than the daytime variety, keeping the baby dry even as she sleeps longer and longer.

1 HAIRBRUSH OR 1 COMB

Look for a soft-bristle brush or a wide-toothed comb that won't snag on tangles or pull your baby's hair.

1 BABY TOOTHBRUSH & BABY TOOTHPASTE

The best toothbrushes for kids have soft bristles that will effectively clean teeth without irritating your child's sensitive gums. Choose a fluoride toothpaste that has no artificial preservatives, colors, or flavors.

SEVERAL BATH TOYS

Bath toys can make bath time enjoyable for you and baby. There are even some fun, educational bath toys.

GET THE RIGHT STUFF!

Go to Simplestbaby.com for recommendations of the smartest baby products and essentials.

INFANT TUB BATHING

1 MONTH

Now that your baby's umbilical cord stump has dried up and fallen off, and your son's circumcision has healed, you can graduate to giving baby full baths using either an infant tub or a baby bath support device in a sink or tub.

BATHING USING BABY BATHTUB

STEP 1

Fill the tub with two to three inches of warm water. Make sure baby's head is supported at all times, and gently lower baby onto the contoured or mesh support of the baby bathtub. The bath temperature for a newborn should be between 95 and 100 degrees Fahrenheit.

STEP 2

To keep the baby warm during the bath, wet a washcloth with the warm water from the tub and drape it across the baby's chest, continuing to moisten it with the warm water from the tub periodically.

STEP 3

Starting with the face, using a second soft washcloth, gently wash. Proceed to washing the body. You can use a tiny bit of baby soap and shampoo to wash each area, and then rinse by pouring warm water from the tub over the area just washed. To rinse the face, use the same washcloth to wipe away any soap. Pay special attention to creases under the arms, behind the ears, around the neck and the genital area where there could be any build up.

WARNING
Never leave a baby unattended in the bath.
Children can drown in less than an inch of water!

STEP 4 Wash the hair toward the end of the bath to keep baby from getting cold. Use a hypoallergenic shampoo to wash the top of his head and hair.

STEP 5 Remove baby from tub and place on a flat, open towel. Wrap baby and dry with the towel. Put a clean diaper on the baby and dress with clothes.

BATHING USING SUPPORT DEVICE

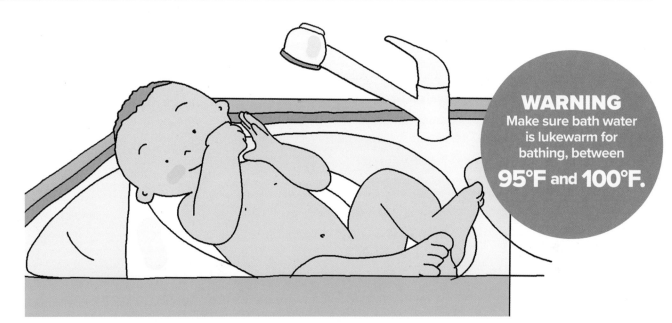

WARNING
Make sure bath water is lukewarm for bathing, between **95°F and 100°F.**

These are ergonomically designed devices that support the baby's body and should have soft, nonslip forms to keep baby from slipping off. Place a bath support device in the sink or bathtub, and then place baby securely on the support.

STEP 1 You can either fill the sink or tub with several inches of water until it slightly covers the legs of the baby or use the faucet to run warm water directly on the baby. **Be extremely careful with the temperature of the water—it should never be more than 100°F (lukewarm to the touch).**

REPEAT STEPS 2, 3, 4, & 5
FROM BATHING USING A BABY BATHTUB

BATHTUB BATHING

6+ MONTHS

There's no fixed rule about when you should stop using the baby bathtub, but most babies are ready for the adult bathtub at around six months, or whenever they're able to sit up well with their own support.

PREPARE AHEAD

Gather all the supplies you will need ahead of the bath, so during the bath you do not need to go and get anything.

LIMIT WATER & TEMPERATURE

Make sure the bathroom is warm and fill the tub with just an inch or two of water. You can add more water as baby grows and is better able to control her body. Test the water before placing your child in it and throughout the bath. It should feel warm but not hot.

BATH WATER SHOULD BE BETWEEN 95°F and 100°F.

NEVER LEAVE BABY UNATTENDED

It takes only a few seconds for a baby to drown, and a baby can drown in as little as one inch of water.

If some distraction comes up while bathing your baby, wrap the baby in a towel and take baby with you. Never put the baby down wrapped in a towel and walk away: loose items like a blanket or towel are suffocation hazards.

SAVING THE BACK

Some parents postpone transitioning to the bathtub because all the bending over can cause back pain and is rough on the knees. If that's the case, use the sink as long as your child still fits.

TWO WAYS TO TRANSITION TO THE TUB

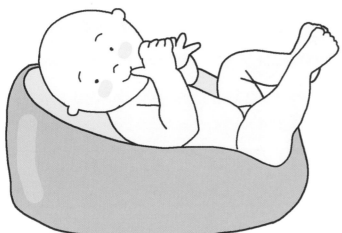

1. USING A SUPPORT DEVICE

Using a formfitting support device allows baby to lie on it in the tub while you wash baby with the bathtub water. It can be a good way to get your baby used to the surroundings of the tub.

2. SITTING PRETTY IN THE TUB

When baby has developed enough strength to sit up well, without any help, usually around six months, she may be ready for her first big girl bath.

As you create your own bath-time ritual, there are some things to note:

- Make sure your baby is always sitting while in the bathtub, being bathed by you.
- Maintain water temperature of between 95°F and 100°F.
- Place a nonslip mat in the tub to prevent accidental falls.
- Get a faucet cover to prevent your baby from bumps and bruises.
- Clear the bathing area from any electrical devices like hair dryers or curling irons.
- Put away any medications.

Daddy Hack
SAVE THE KNEES
Kneeling at the tub can be a real pain. A simple trick is to take a couple of towels or a blanket and fold them over a few times to create a pad for your knees.

OOPS, HOLY CRAP

Yes, it's going to happen. At some point your cute little angel is going to let one go during bath time, and it may happen several times. Here is what to do when it does.

DON'T PANIC!

SHIT HAPPENS TO ALL OF US.

WHAT TO DO WITH POO

OK, so the unthinkable has happened: your baby just took a shit in the tub. Here is what to do:

DON'T PANIC

It's not unusual for babies to poop in the bath, as their bodies are relaxing. If you freak out, they freak out, so stay calm and be reassuring. You don't want baby to develop a negative association with bath time, resulting in baby not wanting to take a bath.

CLEAN UP THE MESS

After taking the baby out of the tub, remove the poop with a plastic baggy and drain the tub. You can use bleach or white vinegar to disinfect the area. Thoroughly rinse the tub after cleaning it. Gather any toys that might have been in the tub and clean them thoroughly too. If they can be safely put in the dishwasher, that is a good way to clean and sterilize the toys.

RE-BATHE THE BABY

Depending on how messy the accident was, you might have to give baby another bath or just a quick sponge bath.

ADJUST FEEDING

If poop deposits in the bath are happening regularly, you might try adjusting baby's feeding time to 20 or 30 minutes earlier.

BE POO-PARED

Consider having the necessary cleaning materials close at hand and something to use to fish out the poo.

Play is life's rehearsal.

PLAY & LEARN

Play is a key part of the healthy growth and development of a baby. It builds baby's motor, sensory, communication, and social–emotional skills. Play is an important way babies learn about the world around them.

DEVELOPMENT
THE MILESTONES

As your baby grows, you will see exciting milestones like smiling, reaching and grabbing, sitting up, and crawling. There are general timelines for when these happen. All babies are different; some babies will reach milestones later than others and be just fine. But if your baby does miss a milestone, be sure to discuss it with your doctor.

THINGS TO NOTE

All babies develop at their own pace, so it's impossible to know exactly when a child will learn a given skill. However, the developmental milestones provide a general guide for when you might expect to see changes.

As a parent, you know your child best. If your child is not meeting the milestones for his or her age, or if you think there could be a problem with your child's development, talk with your child's doctor and share your concerns.

KEY DEVELOPMENTAL MILESTONES

FIRST SMILES — **6–12 WEEKS**

While babies often smile early, it is a result of physical contentment from sleeping, peeing, or passing gas. You can expect baby's first social smile around 6–12 weeks.

GRASPING & REACHING — **3–5 MONTHS**

At the age of three to five months, your baby will begin reaching for and grabbing objects, like favorite toys.

ROLLING OVER — **4–6 MONTHS**

As babies begin to develop stronger neck, back, and abdominal muscles, they will begin rolling over. This happens around four to six months of age. Tummy time exercises help develop the muscles necessary for rolling.

SITTING UP — **7–9 MONTHS**

Babies develop the ability to sit up without help around seven to nine months.

CRAWLING — **6–10 MONTHS**

Babies learn to crawl around 6–10 months. They may start by doing a variation of the standard crawl, like scooting, crab crawling, commando-type crawling, or scooting backward.

FIRST SYLLABLES — **9–11 MONTHS**

Baby's first syllables: sounds like Ma, Da, etc.

WALKING — **9–15 MONTHS**

Babies begin taking those first steps around 9–15 months. Before that happens, you will see the baby pulling up to stand, walking while holding on to furniture, and independently standing alone to take a few steps.

THE MUST-HAVES
PLAY & LEARN

FLOOR MAT | PLAYMAT

As babies begin crawling and taking their first steps, they will also be falling; and a foam floor mat can soften those falls. It also helps with cleaning up spit-ups that can happen during tummy time.

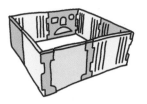

PLAYPEN

When babies get mobile, you may want to contain them at first. Especially if you have to step away for brief moments. A playpen is a small, portable enclosure in which a baby or small child can play safely.

FLOOR GYM

Also known as baby play gym or baby activity gym, this not only offers a variety of sensory activities to encourage development and curiosity in babies, but it is also an excellent area for baby to strengthen the neck and core during tummy time.

BABY TOYS

Look for entertaining, age-appropriate, safe toys for your infant. Painted toys must use lead-free paint. Avoid toys that have small parts that are choking hazards. Make sure that soft plastic toys are phthalates-free.

STUFFED ANIMALS

Stuffed toys should be machine washable and made of fabric labeled flame resistant or flame retardant.

EARLY BOOKS

These help children become familiar with reading and accustomed to listening and focusing. They help instill the joy and fun of reading early on. Reading aloud to your baby also stimulates your baby's language skills and cognitive thinking and enhances memory.

BABY WALKER

Practice makes perfect, and baby walkers are ideal for that. Baby stands up and holds the handle for support while pushing to walk around.

GET THE RIGHT STUFF!

Go to Simplestbaby.com for recommendations of the smartest baby products and essentials.

BABY EXERCISES

Baby exercises strengthen baby's neck, arms, legs, back, and core. They also help develop hand-eye coordination, which helps babies reach developmental milestones like lifting their head, turning over, crawling, and walking.

TUMMY TIME

WHAT IS IT?

Place an awake baby on his stomach in order to help strengthen the infant's neck, back, and shoulder muscles and promote motor skills. **This should always be done only if the baby is being supervised.**

WHY DO IT?

- Helps achieve milestones like rolling over, sitting upright, and crawling
- Boosts gross motor skills
- Engages more muscle groups
- Helps prevent a flat spot on baby's head
- Helps baby achieve better head control
- Helps develop muscle strength, reducing the risk of SIDS

Daddy Hack

Be careful not to do tummy time directly after a feeding or you will be seeing that milk again as spit-up. If you do feed the baby, do a partial feeding and then feed the rest after tummy time.

WHEN TO DO IT?

Tummy time can begin soon after the birth of a healthy baby.

HOW MUCH TO DO?

NEWBORNS: Start with a few minutes a couple of times throughout the day

TWO-MONTH-OLD: 10–15 minute sessions working up to a total of an hour a day

THREE-MONTH-OLD: 10–15 minutes sessions working up to a total of 90 minutes a day

TUMMY-TIME METHODS
3 BEST TECHNIQUES FOR TUMMY TIME
Never leave your baby unattended during tummy time.

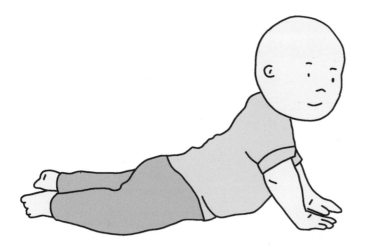

METHOD 1
TRADITIONAL TUMMY TIME
Place baby on his stomach on a flat, clean towel or playmat. Surround baby with a few favorite toys or engage baby with high-contrast toys. For newborns, make sure baby's nose is not being covered and baby can breathe easily while on his tummy.

METHOD 2
PILLOW TUMMY TIME
Fold a pillow slightly over and form it into a U shape. Place baby inside the curve of the pillow, with her arms and shoulders propped on top of the pillow. Hold toys in front of the pillow to keep baby's attention. You can also roll a towel or blanket, bending it into a U shape.

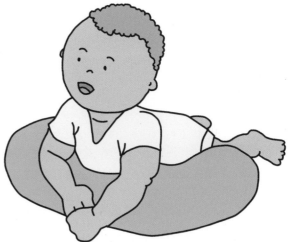

METHOD 3
TUMMY-TO-TUMMY TIME
Lean back while sitting so you are in a reclining position, and place baby on your chest and tummy. Hold the baby in place with your hands while in this position. This can be easier for young newborns until they are stronger.

BABY EXERCISES

Baby exercises are an important part of infant development. Infant exercise helps strengthen baby's neck and develop hand-eye coordination, ultimately helping baby learn to walk. It also builds muscles, joints, and bones and improves coordination, balance, and flexibility.

Daddy Hack

Printing out black-and-white art and attaching it to the under side of the top of the floor gym structure can help engage baby. Babies can't see in color until around five months but enjoy contrast.

FLOOR GYMS | TUMMY TIME

These fun and colorful structures are designed to encourage babies to reach and grasp for objects. They also help with the development of hand-eye coordination and can also be used to do tummy-time exercises.

BABY SIT-UPS

Helping baby rise up into a sitting position is another good way to strengthen the core, arms, neck, and back muscles.

Place baby on his back on a flat surface and grasp him by the elbows and forearms.

Gently raise baby up toward you into a sitting position. Hold him in the position for 5–10 seconds.

Then slowly lower baby back down, pausing when you almost reach the bottom to let him try to engage his muscles.

You can do this three to five minutes at a time, two to three times a day.

NOTE:

Your baby should already have the strength to support his head before attempting to do this exercise.

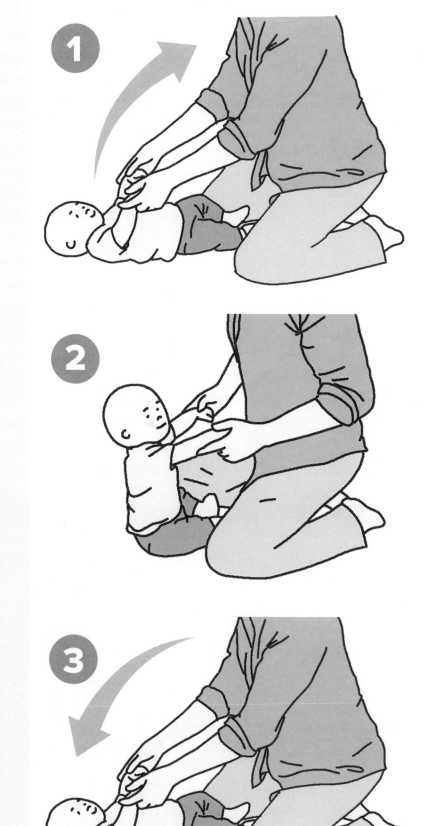

SOCIALIZATION
NICE TO MEET YOU, BABY

For many new parents, the desire to socialize baby may be spurred by their own need to get out and see other adults. Whether it's in the form of classes, playdates, or childcare, social activities play an important role in baby's development. Babies can build social skills and confidence. If you are ready to venture out with baby, here's some helpful advice.

FAMILY MEMBERS

The socialization of a baby begins at birth with your skin-to-skin contact, breast-feeding, and cuddling with family and caregivers. These are all ways that babies learn the social cues and discover the world around them.

PLAYGROUPS

When baby is still an infant, playgroups are opportunities for you to connect with other parents who are experiencing similar things and build a support network.

Babies don't play with other babies in the traditional sense. They engage in what is called solitary play, in which babies play independently. Babies do enjoy the company of other babies but, more importantly, these groups give baby a chance to discover new environments and play with different toys.

Providing baby with a variety of social opportunities is the best way to begin developing her social skills—so get out there and play.

COVID-19 NOTE:
Traditional playgroups may be affected by the current infectious disease environment, so it's important to consult your doctor regarding what is safe for you and your baby. You will need to look at what the experts say, weigh the risks, and decide your level of comfort.

IDEAS FOR SOCIALIZATION

- Join a parent or baby playgroup.

- Take a "mommy or daddy and me" class.

- Organize playdates.

- Set up a weekly time to meet at the park.

- Join a baby gym.

- Become a member of a children's museum, zoo, or aquarium.

- Consider a parent–baby fitness group or baby yoga class.

- Sign up for a baby music program.

SUPER BABY
BUILDING CONFIDENCE IN INFANTS

We all want our children to be healthy, happy, and confident. We've all seen little ones who bump into something, are startled, or don't get what they want, and start screaming like the world is coming to an end. Not to mention children who are so timid they hang on to their parents' legs for dear life.

START EARLY

Putting the building blocks of confidence in place is important even though baby is just a little one. It's from those early steps that your baby is put on the path to becoming the little superhero.

SUPERHERO IN TRAINING
TIPS FOR BUILDING SELF-CONFIDENCE

ENCOURAGE CURIOSITY

Confidence in babies is often expressed by willingness to explore. You have to be willing not only to let them but also to encourage them. Babies taking those first adventurous steps to explore will look to you for reassurance.

DON'T OVERREACT

We all have the inclination to step in as soon as baby takes a tumble or bumps his head, knee, etc. But you are not helping if you overreact, fuss, and pick up baby over little bumps and bruises.

Of course, you should take care of baby to prevent more serious accidents; we're talking about little things. Responding appropriately to the situation is as important as managing your reactions, since babies take cues from their parents.

PLAY WITH THEM

The simple act of being there and playing with baby provides a sense of security and importance. It is essential for babies to feel confident and safe.

RESPOND TO THEM

Your response to baby's communication is key. Talking to her, listening, and making eye contact gives baby needed reassurance.

SHOWER BABY WITH LOVE

Showing lots and lots of affection to your baby is one of the most powerful things you can do. You can never give too many hugs, smiles, and kisses, as they demonstrate that your baby is loved and valued.

ESTABLISH A ROUTINE

Babies tend to be more confident when they are in a routine and begin to know what to expect, so establishing a routine for things like bedtime, feeding, etc. is helpful.

LET THEM DO IT

Help babies become good problem solvers by letting them solve problems, like lifting a hidden object in a storybook or putting a block in a slot. You may show them, but you should also let them do it themselves.

Taking care
of baby is
one of the
most important
jobs in life.

BABY CARE

There are lots of things to be aware of now that you have a little one to look after.
Don't worry, we have addressed some of the basic baby-care issues you will need to know
and how to handle them.

THE MUST-HAVES
TO HANDLE BASIC BABY-CARE NEEDS

1 NAIL CLIPPER OR SCISSORS

Designed specifically for baby, use nail scissors with blunt, rounded tips or baby nail clippers that are designed to prevent nicking the tip of baby's finger or toe.

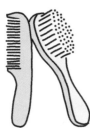

1 COMB & 1 BRUSH

All you need is a soft-bristled baby brush or baby comb—a detangling brush is best.

1 TOOTHBRUSH

Find one with super-soft bristles and made of BPA- and phthalate-free material. You can use a traditional infant toothbrush or a finger toothbrush.

TOOTHPASTE

The American Academy of Pediatric Dentistry (AAPD) recommends using cavity-preventing fluoride toothpaste starting with baby's very first tooth.

EMERY BOARD

There are nail files specifically made for babies, but you can also use your own.

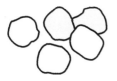

1 BAG OF COTTON BALLS

These small balls of cotton can be used for cleaning baby.

1 BOTTLE OF RUBBING ALCOHOL

70 percent isopropyl alcohol liquid; used primarily as a topical antiseptic.

GET THE RIGHT STUFF!
Go to Simplestbaby.com for recommendations of the smartest baby products and essentials.

CORD CARE

The umbilical cord is the source of food and oxygen for baby throughout pregnancy. Once it is cut, what is left is a purplish-blue stump around one-half inch long. It takes one to three weeks for this stump to dry up and fall off. During that time, it will require care and attention to prevent irritation and infection.

TIPS FOR CARING FOR THE CORD

KEEP IT DRY

During baby's first few weeks, don't wash the cord or get it wet. Expose it to as much air as possible to help it dry out. Keep the front of your baby's diaper folded down so it doesn't cover the stump.

SPONGE BATHS

During the first couple of weeks, you will give your newborn sponge baths, rather than a bath in a baby tub, to help keep the cord dry. If you need to clean the stump, do so gently using a cotton swab or Q-tip dipped in 70 percent isopropyl alcohol.

ALLOW IT TO HEAL NATURALLY

Resist the temptation to remove the drying cord; allow it to fall off naturally. During the healing process, it's normal to see a little blood near the stump. Much like a scab, the cord stump might bleed a little when it falls off.

WHAT IS AN OUTIE BELLY BUTTON?

Once the cord dries up and falls off, the belly button still protrudes out rather than receding in. This is not caused by how the cord is clamped or cut. There is no medical concern with baby having an outie belly button, and about 10 percent of the population has them.

WHEN TO CALL THE DOCTOR

Signs of infection

- Redness or swelling of the area

- Continues to bleed

- Oozes yellowish discharge

- Has a foul-smelling odor

- Discomfort for baby when the stump is touched

- Fever

Actively Bleeding

Bleeding normally occurs, but active bleeding is defined by wiping a drop of blood and another drop appears.

UMBILICAL CORD GRANULOMA

An umbilical granuloma is a common small nodule of red tissue that has a small amount of yellow-green discharge. It's different from an infection in that it is not accompanied by swelling, redness, or fever.

This can resolve itself, but if it persists, your doctor may treat it by cauterization. This is performed by applying silver nitrate to the area to burn the tissue. This does not cause the baby any pain, as there are no nerve endings in this area.

The information provided is not a substitute for professional medical advice, diagnosis, or treatment. Always consult your pediatrician or health-care provider to ensure that a treatment is right for you and your child.

TRIMMING NAILS

Trimming your baby's nails can be a scary thing to do. Those fingers are so small and just don't want to stop moving. Baby's nails are pretty soft but can also be pretty sharp! Newborns tend to have flailing arms, which can result in scratches to their little faces. Fingernails might require cutting or filing a couple of times a week, whereas toenails need less frequent trimming.

TIPS FOR TRIMMING BABY'S NAILS

CHECK FOR LONG NAILS

Run your finger upward over the front of the nail—if it feels long or sharp, it will need trimming.

FILE THEM

During those first couple weeks of a new baby's life, the nails are very soft and should be filed with an emery board to smooth the edges, rather than cut.

FIND SOME LIGHT

Find a well-lit place to do the trimming so you can clearly see what you are doing.

GET THE RIGHT EQUIPMENT

Using baby nail clippers or nail scissors is safer and easier than using those made for adults. You may begin using a clipper after one month.

THE RIGHT TIME

Wait until your baby is sleeping to clip his nails. If you're lucky, your baby will sleep right through it. If you have to do it while he is awake, distract him with a toy, possibly giving it to him in the opposite hand you are trimming.

TRIMMING BABY'S NAILS

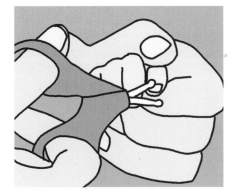

BABY SCISSORS

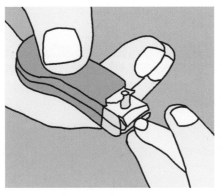

BABY CLIPPERS

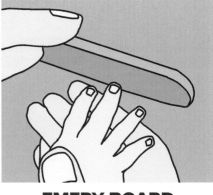

EMERY BOARD

TRIMMING

After the first month, baby's nails become harder and will be easier to cut. Before then, you should smooth down the nails by using an emery board.

To trim, hold the baby's hand firmly, pulling the finger pad back and slightly away from the nail to avoid nicking the skin. Very carefully cut the fingernails along the curve of the finger. It is recommended you do this in three cuts that follow the natural curve of the nail. When using baby scissors, you can usually do this in one cut.

SMOOTH OUT THE EDGES

After trimming your baby's nails, you will want to smooth out the sharp edges using an emery board.

FIRST AID

Nicking your baby's tiny fingers is awful, but don't feel too bad; it happens pretty much to everyone. Rinse the cut under cool water, hold a sterile pad or cotton ball to the finger, and apply a little pressure. The bleeding usually stops in a couple of minutes.

Never use a bandage on a baby's finger. It's likely to come off when baby puts her finger in her mouth, which can be a choking hazard.

FIRST HAIRCUT

How much hair and how fast it grows determines when your baby will need a first haircut. Here are some helpful tips for getting through it without a meltdown.

FIRST TRIM OPTIONS

DIY

If you feel up to it, you could give your baby that first trim yourself.

KIDDIE SALON

Children's salons are designed to work with young children to make it fun; they are often equipped with toys and videos to distract them.

DIY HAIR-CUTTING TIPS

PREPARE AHEAD

Get everything you need ahead of time
- The chair (ideally, a high chair)
- A comb or brush
- Hair clippers
- Scissors
- Towels or smock
- Spray water bottle

Find a location where you have the TV or iPad set up to keep baby entertained, and have his favorite toys ready.

SETTING THINGS UP

With baby in his chair, drape a towel around baby's shoulders and secure with a hair clip. If that does not work, then skip it. You can always just change his outfit after the trim.

TRIMMING

Dampen baby's hair with water from a spray bottle, and comb the hair flat. Start trimming section by section. Using two fingers, slide your fingers through the hair, moving it away from baby's head. When you reach the length you like, trim with the scissors. Always keep your fingers between the scissors and the baby's head.

QUICK TIP

Remember to save those first locks of hair for your baby's memory book and take lots of pictures and video.

TIPS FOR BABY'S FIRST SALON CUT

TIMING HELPS

Book an appointment between mealtime and naptime, so your baby isn't hungry or cranky. Call ahead to make sure the stylist is running on time, and don't hesitate to reschedule if your baby seems out of sorts that day.

TAKE A SEAT

If baby is having difficulty sitting in the stylist's chair, try sitting baby on your lap.

ROUTINE IS KEY

Going for regular haircuts with the same stylist is helpful for your child's next haircut, as it will help your child build trust and familiarity.

CONTROL THE VIEW

Before the stylist begins, you might want to swing the chair around so your baby is not looking in the mirror at the stylist and scissors.

BRING DISTRACTIONS

Consider bringing your baby's favorite small toy or stuffed animal. Having some treats and your iPad with your baby's favorite videos can help too.

EXTRA OUTFIT

If your baby refuses to wear the cape, you might want to have an extra change of clothes.

KEEP YOUR COOL

If you're nervous, your baby will pick up on it; keep your cool.

BRUSHING BABY'S TEETH

Baby teeth may be small, but they're important. They act as placeholders for adult teeth. Without a healthy set of baby teeth, your child can have trouble chewing and speaking clearly. That's why caring for baby teeth and keeping them decay-free is so important.

WHEN TEETH APPEAR

Babies start getting their first teeth between 4 and 10 months.

CHOOSING A TOOTHBRUSH

The best toothbrush for kids has soft, rounded bristles, which will effectively clean teeth without irritating your baby's sensitive gums. Choose a toothbrush that is sized appropriately to little hands and mouths.

The brush should have:
- Soft bristles
- A small, round head
- A large handle
- And be child-size

Daddy Hack

Starting an early routine of brushing your baby's teeth can help little ones get into the habit of doing it; so when it's time for your child to do it himself, it goes smoother.

WHAT ABOUT FLUORIDE?

The American Academy of Pediatrics recommends using a small amount of fluoride toothpaste that is the size of a grain of rice for children under the age of three, and a pea-sized amount for a child older than three.

STAGES OF DENTAL HYGIENE

6 MONTHS

As baby's first teeth pop out, you can start cleaning them with a soft washcloth. Using a small amount of water and toothpaste, wipe the teeth or use a finger brush. It is recommended that you clean baby's teeth once a day.

9 MONTHS

You can introduce a child-sized toothbrush at this time. Brush gently all around your child's baby teeth, front and back. You will be brushing your baby's teeth until he or she is old enough to hold the brush. Use kids' fluoride toothpaste, about the size of a grain of rice on the brush.

18 MONTHS

At 18 months, you may still be the one doing the brushing, but you should begin letting your child try too. Begin to encourage your child to spit out toothpaste after brushing, but not to rinse.

3 YEARS

Start using a pea-sized amount of low-fluoride toothpaste to brush your child's teeth. Continue to supervise the process until your child can rinse and spit without assistance. Keep an eye out for any signs of baby tooth decay, brown or white spots, or pits on the teeth.

NATURAL BOY
(UNCIRCUMCISED)
TAKING CARE OF HIS EQUIPMENT

WHAT IS IT?

Uncircumcised means you did not remove the foreskin covering the head of your baby boy's penis.

HOW TO CARE FOR IT

In the first few months, you should simply clean and bathe your baby's uncircumcised penis with soap and water, like the rest of the diaper area. No special cleansing of the penis with cotton swabs or antiseptics is necessary, but you should observe your baby urinating to confirm there is no blockage of the stream due to the hole in the foreskin being too small.

WHEN TO CONTACT THE DOCTOR

If the pee stream is consistently no more than a trickle, or if your baby seems to have some discomfort while urinating, contact your doctor.

RETRACTING THE FORESKIN
DON'T DO IT!

The doctor will tell you when the foreskin has separated and can be retracted safely. Don't ever try to pull back the foreskin to clean under it because, in a newborn baby, it's fused to the head of the penis, and forcing it back can cause pain or bleeding.

WHAT IT LOOKS LIKE

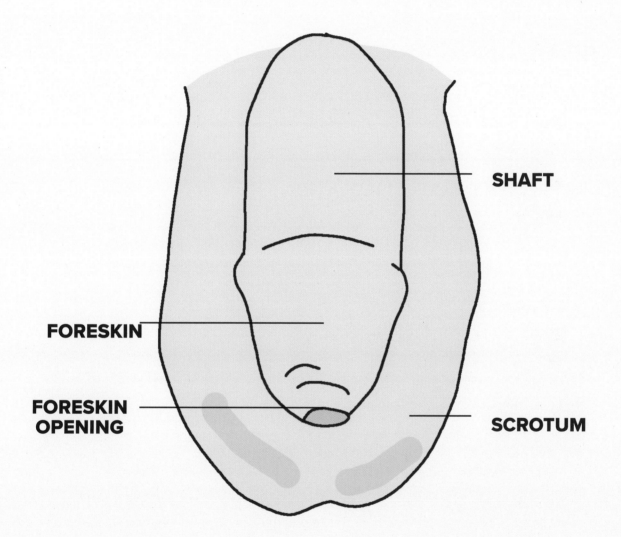

SHAFT

FORESKIN

FORESKIN
OPENING

SCROTUM

SNIP SNIP
(CIRCUMCISED)
TAKING CARE OF HIS EQUIPMENT

WHAT IS IT?

All boys are born with a piece of skin, called the foreskin, covering the head of their penis. Circumcision is a procedure in which this skin is removed; it is usually performed within the first couple of days after birth, in the hospital or at a religious ceremony.

CARING FOR A CIRCUMCISED PENIS

SWELLING

You will notice redness and swelling behind or under the head of the penis and possibly some yellow secretion; this is normal and should improve in a week.

BLEEDING

Blood staining of the diaper is common after circumcision. During the first 24 hours, check the diaper at every change for active bleeding. It is normal to see spots of blood no bigger than a quarter (about an inch wide), but you should see a doctor if there is more blood.

KEEP IT CLEAN

Make sure the wound and penis are kept as clean as possible. At every diaper change, gently wipe away any poop on the area. Use a hypoallergenic, fragrance-free soap and warm water to clean. Allow it to dry on its own. Avoid any strong rubbing.

KEEP AN EYE ON IT

If the tip of your baby's circumcised penis is a little red, and appears bruised, it's okay. The glans may have off-white or yellowish patches in the first few days. These are a type of scab and are completely normal.

The information provided is not a substitute for professional medical advice, diagnosis, or treatment. Always consult your pediatrician or health-care provider to ensure that a treatment is right for you and your child.

PAIN RELIEF

Signs of pain can include crying and problems with sleeping and feeding. During the first 24 hours after your baby's circumcision, you may be directed by your doctor to give acetaminophen to help manage your baby's pain.

PROTECT IT

A bandage with petroleum jelly may be placed on the penis after surgery. Check with your doctor about whether or not to continue putting a dressing over a healing penis.

Either way, you should apply a dab of petroleum jelly or antibiotic ointment after every diaper change to protect and keep the penis from sticking to and rubbing against the diaper.

SYMPTOMS OF CONCERN

Should your baby show any of the following symptoms, contact your doctor:

- Trouble peeing
- Bleeding or blood on diaper bigger than a quarter
- Worsening swelling and redness for more than five days
- Yellow discharge lasting more than a week
- Foul-smelling drainage
- Fever
- Crusty, fluid-filled sores
- After two weeks, the plastic ring used for circumcision hasn't fallen off

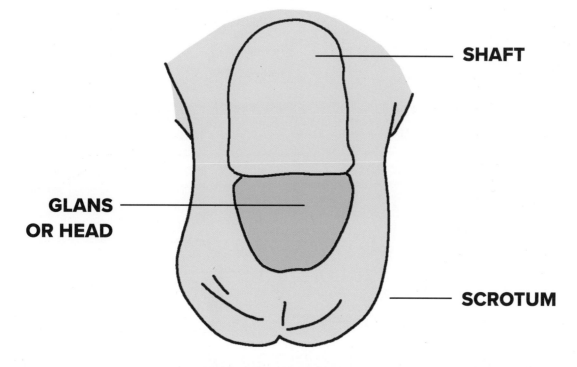

Behind every
baby is a basket
of laundry.

CLOTHING
ESSENTIALS

Everything you need to know to understand clothing, sizing, and care

SIZING THINGS UP

Babies come in all shapes and sizes and grow at different rates, so finding the right size for your little one can be tricky. Sizing charts are intended to give a general guide for infant sizes based on the weight and height of most children.

BABY APPAREL SIZE CHART

SIZE	WEIGHT	HEIGHT
Newborn	6–9 lb.	up to 19 inches
0–3M	9–12 lb.	19–23 inches
3–6M	12–17 lb.	23–25 inches
6–9M	17–20 lb.	25–27 inches
9–12M	20–22 lb.	27–29 inches
12–18M	22–27 lb.	29–31 inches
18–24M	27–30 lb.	31–33 inches

WASHING TIPS

PREWASH

Part of the manufacturing process involves the use of chemicals and finishing agents that could potentially cause babies' sensitive skin to be irritated or get a rash. The clothing could also have picked up dirt and/or germs at retail. It's best to err on the safe side and wash everything before you put it on your baby.

USE DETERGENTS THAT ARE

- Paraben-free
- Phthalate-free
- Dye-free
- No artificial brighteners
- Fragrance-free
- Hypoallergenic
- Phosphate-free
- Nontoxic
- Fluoride-free

THE MUST-HAVES

NEWBORN CLOTHING

NB

The clothing you will need for a newborn isn't much. Keep in mind that babies grow quickly and the newborn stage will not last long, so we recommend just the essentials.

QUICK TIP

Onesies have little flaps on their shoulders. They are meant to help you slide the onesie down baby's legs rather than pulling it over baby's head. This can make changing a poop explosion far far less messy.

NEWBORN OUTFIT ESSENTIALS

6
ONESIES

Look for organic 100 percent cotton. Ideally ones with wide head-and-leg openings and a minimum number of snaps. Depending on the weather, you might also consider a couple of long-sleeve onesies.

2–3
HATS

You might need both a wide-brimmed hat for summer and one that covers baby's ears in winter.

3–4
PAIRS OF SOCKS

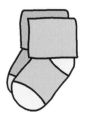

You will run through more socks than ever. A variety of socks can be fun, but if you keep to a general color palette, they will be easier to match with outfits.

5

SLEEP OUTFITS

ROMPER

Look for one-piece sleep outfits. We recommend the version with zippers, not snaps or buttons. It should not be too loose, to prevent the baby from slipping out of it.

SWEATER, COAT, OR DRESS

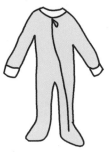

These articles of clothing may not be essential for everyone, but if you are in a cold climate, having a coat or sweater for your newborn is helpful. Dresses are nice, but we recommend not going overboard as your newborns will grow out of them very quickly.

Daddy Hack

If you are considering having more than one child, think about buying unisex white onesies, white socks, etc., so that you can use them for your second or third child.

GET THE RIGHT STUFF!

Go to Simplestbaby.com for recommendations of the smartest baby products and essentials.

THE MUST-HAVES

INFANT CLOTHING

Some of the things you will need for your infant are similar to what you need for a newborn, but bigger. You will also start to get additional clothing that is similar to what an adult would wear. Some of these things will be driven by how much you are willing to spend.

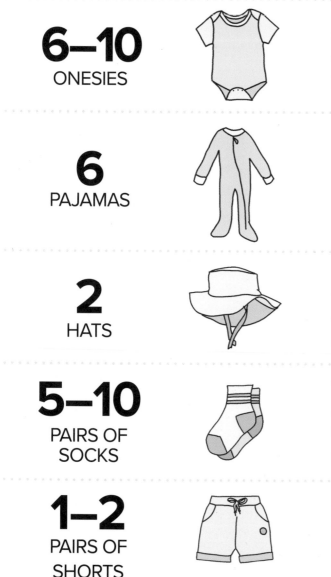

6–10 ONESIES

Onesies will be a staple of your baby's wardrobe for a good year and maybe well beyond.

6 PAJAMAS

Look for one-piece sleep outfits. We recommend the version with zippers, not snaps or buttons. They should not be too loose, to prevent the baby from slipping out of them.

2 HATS

Depending on where you live, you might want to get a hat for summer and one for winter: a wide-brimmed hat for summer and one that covers baby's ears for winter.

5–10 PAIRS OF SOCKS

You will run through more socks than ever. A variety of socks can be fun, but if you keep them in a general color palette, they will be easier to match with outfits.

1–2 PAIRS OF SHORTS

Shorts are a good addition to the little one's wardrobe.

2–3
T-SHIRTS

You will start using T-shirts the closer your baby gets to 12 months. You will likely use a mix of onesies and T-shirts.

3
PANTS OR LEGGINGS

You will need pants for boys and leggings and pants for girls.

1–2
COATS

This purchase will be influenced by the weather where you live—a light jacket and something a bit heavier for cold-climate areas.

3
DRESSES

This is more for parents than for the baby. If you really want to put your little sweetheart in dresses, then you might want more. We received incredible designer dresses as gifts, and our little girl grew out of them before she even had a chance to wear them.

1–2
SWEATERS

Sweaters depend on the climate where you live. You probably will need at least one for those chilly days or nights and air-conditioned rooms.

2–3
PAIRS OF SHOES

You will likely buy more of these when the baby starts getting mobile, but it is nice to have a couple of pairs when you go out with your baby.

GET THE RIGHT STUFF!
Go to Simplestbaby.com for recommendations of the smartest baby products and essentials.

THE MUST-HAVES

TODDLER CLOTHING

Your child will be learning to walk and will be more active than ever. It's go, go, go, so you will be running through clothes faster than ever. Durability is important as your baby puts those outfits to the test and you try to keep up with washing.

6
ONESIES

Onesies will be a staple of your baby's wardrobe for a good year and maybe well beyond.

6
PAJAMAS

You will continue to use one-piece pajamas. As your baby nears one year of age, you may begin to add some two-piece sleep outfits.

2
HATS

Depending on where you live, you might want to get a hat for summer and one for winter: a wide-brimmed hat for summer and one that covers baby's ears for winter.

5–10
PAIRS OF
SOCKS

You will run through more socks than ever. A variety of socks can be fun, but if you keep them in some general color palette, they will be easier to match with outfits.

4–5
T-SHIRTS

Look for cotton T-shirts and turtlenecks with snaps at the neck that will slip easily over your baby's head. Undershirts are an easy way to add a layer of warmth.

5–6
PANTS OR LEGGINGS

You will be getting a variety of pants for your toddler, some with zippers, some with buttons, and some with elastic, which are good for kids who are learning to potty train.

2–3
SHORTS

Shorts are a good addition to the little one's wardrobe.

1–2
COATS

A fleece jacket with a hood is a cozy and efficient way to bundle up your child; a hoodie or jean jacket is great for a lighter cover-up.

3–4
DRESSES

Now that your little one is a bit older, you will need more casual dresses and maybe some nicer ones for special occasions.

1–2
SWEATERS

Depending on the climate where you live, you potentially will need at least several for those chilly days or nights.

4–6
PAIRS OF SHOES

More mobile means more shoes. You will be using a lot more shoes at this time: gym shoes, sandals, loafer slip-ons, etc., as style is coming more and more into play.

1–2
SWIMSUITS

Now that your toddler may begin swimming lessons or playing in a small pool, you will need a durable swimsuit that is easy to get on and off.

1
SNOWSUIT

Depending on the climate where you live, you might invest in a snowsuit and gear.

GET THE RIGHT STUFF!
Go to Simplestbaby.com for recommendations of the smartest baby products and essentials.

Safety is no accident.

SAFETY

Child safety is one of the top priorities for a parent. This section covers tips to help make sure that your baby's world is as safe and fun as possible.

THE MUST-HAVES

HOME CHILDPROOFING

Once babies are on the move, there's no stopping their curiosity! They will be getting into everything. To keep your little one safe, you'll need to do some babyproofing. Here is what you will need:

CABINET LOCKS

These devices prevent little children from opening cabinets.

SOCKET COVERS

Electrical socket safety covers are designed to prevent children from tampering with the outlet and from being shocked or even electrocuted.

CORNER COVERS

These devices are used to cover sharp corners of tables, doorways, and even around fireplaces. These come in different sizes and configurations depending on the need.

STAIR | DOOR GATES

These devices are used to block or prevent children from entering a particular area that could be dangerous, or from exiting a safe area.

OVEN LOCK

These locks keep the oven closed so it can't be opened by curious little children.

STOVE KNOB COVERS

These are clear plastic covers that fit over your stove knobs to prevent children from turning on the stove.

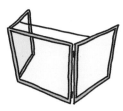

FIREPLACE LOCK | COVER

These devices mount over the handles of swinging or folding doors to lock them in place and prevent a child from pinching their fingers in the door. The cover blocks the fireplace to prevent children from getting into it.

DOOR-HANDLE COVERS

These devices fit over the doorknob and spin loosely around the knob when a child tries to turn it. By squeezing the two grab-tabs together, you are able to open the door.

SMOKE DETECTOR

Smoke detectors are used to detect if there is a fire and sets off an alarm in the home. They can be configured to notify the fire department as well.

CARBON MONOXIDE DETECTOR

This detector (CO detector) is a device that warns you of the presence of carbon monoxide gas, preventing carbon monoxide poisoning. These should be placed in the hallway outside the bedrooms.

FIRE EXTINGUISHER

Home fire extinguishers are classified either A, B, or C (or a combination of these) to indicate which types of fires they will work on: combustible, chemical, or electrical. General household extinguishers are called universal extinguishers or ABC extinguishers.

TOILET LATCH

This is a device used to keep young children from opening the toilet to prevent accidental drowning. You can avoid using these if you can keep bathroom doors closed with door-handle covers on the knobs.

GET THE RIGHT STUFF!

Go to Simplestbaby.com for recommendations of the smartest baby products and essentials.

CHILD-PROOFING
THE NURSERY

SMOKE DECTECTOR
Install and test it regularly. Be sure to replace the batteries at least once a year.

ANCHOR FURNITURE
Anchor dressers and bookshelves to walls with braces to prevent them from toppling over onto your child. Keep toddlers from climbing up open dresser drawers by securing them with childproof locks.

GATES
Prevent late-night walkabouts by installing a baby gate or door with handle covers to prevent toddlers from opening the door.

OUTLETS
Put plastic outlet protectors over all unused electrical outlets.

VENTING
Keep your baby from overheating, which is a known risk factor associated with SIDS; never place a crib next to a heater or in an area of direct sunlight.

MATTRESS | BEDDING
Must be firm and fit the crib properly. There should be no more than two fingers width of space between the side of the mattress and the crib frame. Use only a fitted sheet and fitted water-resistant mattress cover.

RUGS
Place nonslip pads under all area rugs.

Don't hang anything, for example, mirrors and large frames, over the crib. They could fall and injure your baby.

MOBILES
Remove crib mobiles, especially once your child can stand.

Position crib away from windows and other furniture in case your child attempts to climb out of the crib. Install window stops to prevent windows from opening more than a few inches. Remove or tie up window blind cords as they pose a strangulation hazard.

No blankets, pillows, bumpers, or plush toys should be placed in the crib. These items all pose a risk of suffocation or entrapment and should never be used in a baby's crib.

CRIBS
Should be sturdy with fixed sides and slats spaced no more than 2³/₈ inches apart and made of eco-friendly sustainable materials and nontoxic paint. Headboards should not have decorative cutouts or embellishments that clothing could catch on.

ROCKER | GLIDER
Protect little toes and fingers by choosing a glider with a stop-lock mechanism that prevents the chair from gliding when not in use, and be sure that all gears are encased and out of reach.

CHILD-PROOFING KITCHEN

GLASSES | DISHES
Keep dishware and glasses out of reach of little ones.

KNIVES
Keep knives and kitchen utensils away and out of reach of little ones.

SMALL APPLIANCES
Keep small appliances unplugged when not in use.

CABINETS
Install safety latches on cabinets and cupboards that hold anything that could be dangerous or harmful to children.

DISHWASHER
Putting a latch on the door can help keep out curious toddlers. Place forks and knives in the dishwasher with the handles up and sharp parts pointing down.

TABLECLOTHS
Don't use placemats or tablecloths because a child can pull them and what's on top of them down and hurt himself.

SHARP CORNERS
Install protective corner guards or cushions on the surfaces with sharp corners to prevent head or eye injury.

CLEANING AGENTS
Keep detergents, pesticides, cleaning products, and any other toxic household chemicals locked up in a high cabinet.

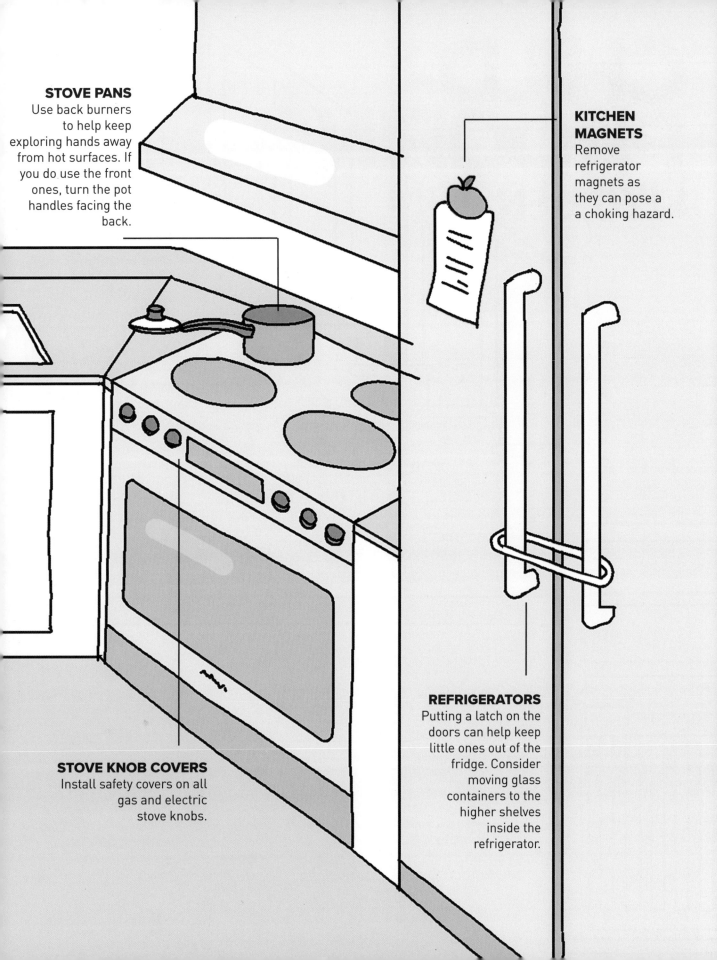

STOVE PANS
Use back burners to help keep exploring hands away from hot surfaces. If you do use the front ones, turn the pot handles facing the back.

KITCHEN MAGNETS
Remove refrigerator magnets as they can pose a a choking hazard.

STOVE KNOB COVERS
Install safety covers on all gas and electric stove knobs.

REFRIGERATORS
Putting a latch on the doors can help keep little ones out of the fridge. Consider moving glass containers to the higher shelves inside the refrigerator.

CHILD-PROOFING
LIVING ROOM

FLOOR LAMPS

Remove, or move floor lamps that could tip over behind furniture where they will be out of reach.

ELECTRICAL OUTLETS

Cover all electrical outlets with safety plugs.

BABY GATE

Place gates at the bottom and top of staircases and where necessary to prevent baby from wandering into danger.

SHARP CORNERS

Use corner guards on all tables and furniture that has sharp corners.

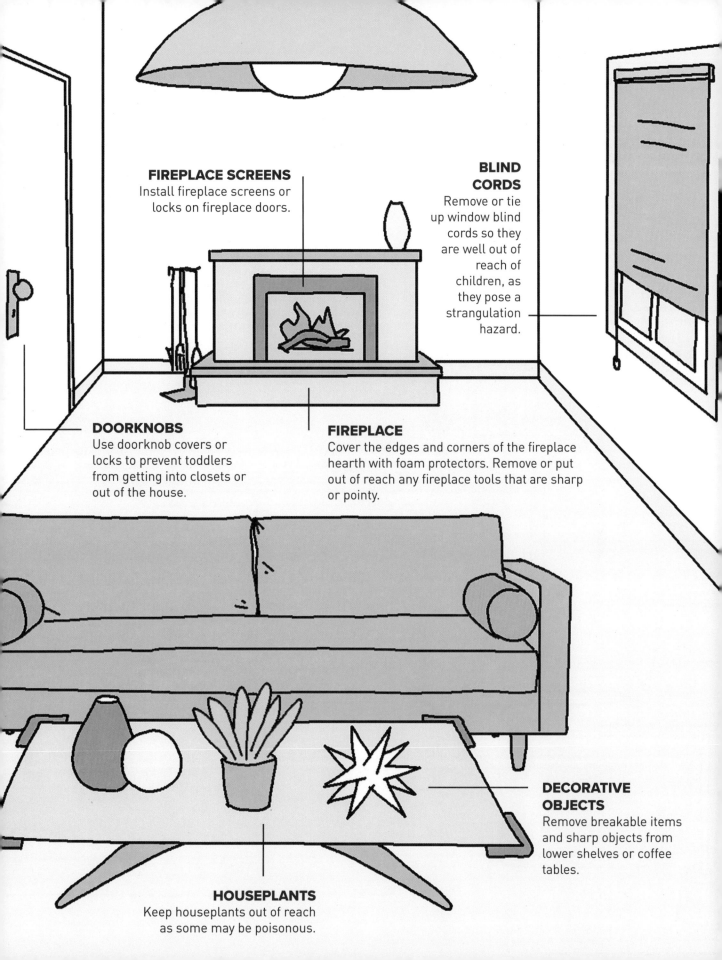

FIREPLACE SCREENS
Install fireplace screens or locks on fireplace doors.

BLIND CORDS
Remove or tie up window blind cords so they are well out of reach of children, as they pose a strangulation hazard.

DOORKNOBS
Use doorknob covers or locks to prevent toddlers from getting into closets or out of the house.

FIREPLACE
Cover the edges and corners of the fireplace hearth with foam protectors. Remove or put out of reach any fireplace tools that are sharp or pointy.

DECORATIVE OBJECTS
Remove breakable items and sharp objects from lower shelves or coffee tables.

HOUSEPLANTS
Keep houseplants out of reach as some may be poisonous.

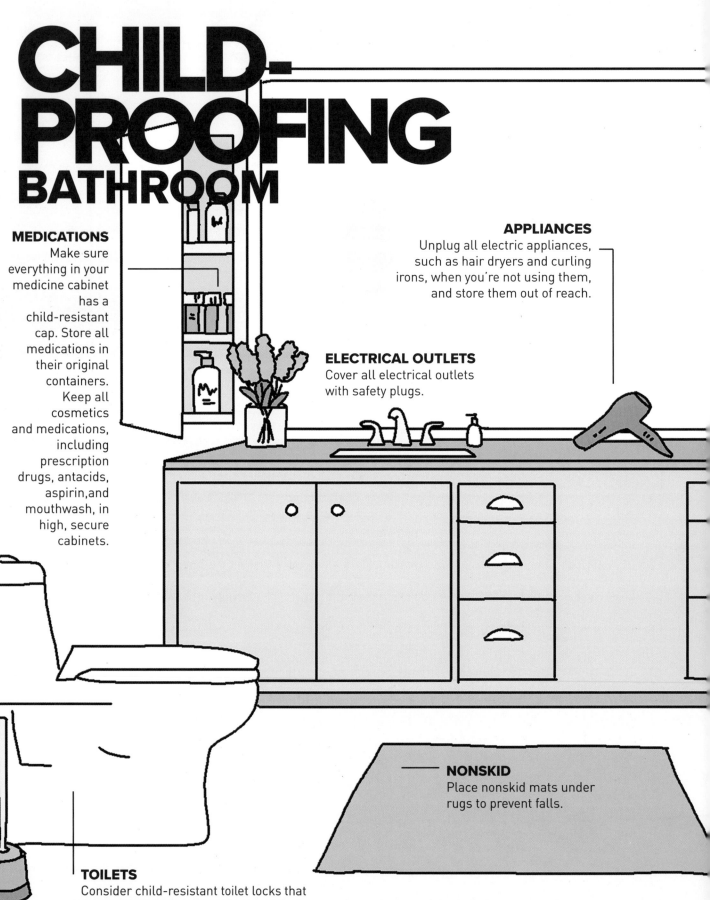

CHILD-PROOFING
BATHROOM

MEDICATIONS
Make sure everything in your medicine cabinet has a child-resistant cap. Store all medications in their original containers. Keep all cosmetics and medications, including prescription drugs, antacids, aspirin, and mouthwash, in high, secure cabinets.

APPLIANCES
Unplug all electric appliances, such as hair dryers and curling irons, when you're not using them, and store them out of reach.

ELECTRICAL OUTLETS
Cover all electrical outlets with safety plugs.

NONSKID
Place nonskid mats under rugs to prevent falls.

TOILETS
Consider child-resistant toilet locks that secure the lid when the toilet is not in use.

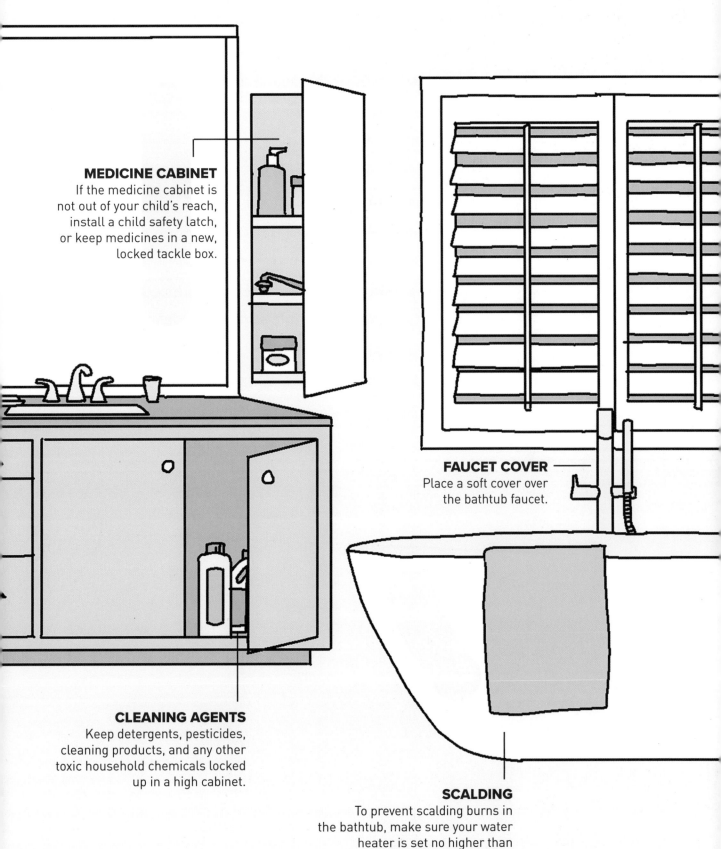

MEDICINE CABINET
If the medicine cabinet is not out of your child's reach, install a child safety latch, or keep medicines in a new, locked tackle box.

FAUCET COVER
Place a soft cover over the bathtub faucet.

CLEANING AGENTS
Keep detergents, pesticides, cleaning products, and any other toxic household chemicals locked up in a high cabinet.

SCALDING
To prevent scalding burns in the bathtub, make sure your water heater is set no higher than 120 degrees Fahrenheit.

CHILD-PROOFING
THE BACKYARD

REMOVE | COVER FIRE PITS
Cover or remove pits to prevent children from burning themselves. Use sand in place of glass in fire pits.

PAD FURNITURE
Cover exposed edges of outdoor furniture, especially tables, which often have sharp corners.

POOL & HOT TUB SAFETY
The AAP recommendation is to enclose the perimeter of swimming pools with a fence.

Most hot tubs will come with their own cover, so make sure it has a security lock and is engaged.

CHECK PLANTS
Dig up and remove any toxic plants in the yard so your child doesn't ingest them. Examples of toxic plants inclu azalea, barberry, calla lily, holly, and oleander. If you have cacti with spines in your yard, you might consider removing them, too.

FENCING

Fence in all or part of the yard to create a safe play area for your child. The fence keeps your child away from danger, like the street, and prevents the child from wandering off.

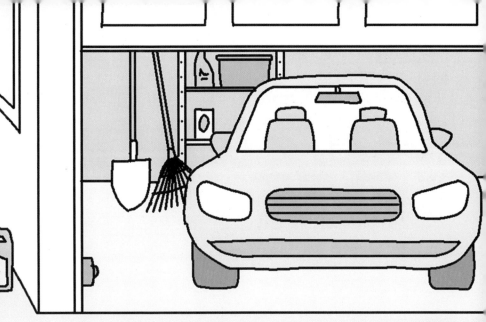

LAWN CHEMICALS

Lock up lawn chemicals such as weed killer, lawn fertilizer, pesticides, rusty paint cans, etc. Make sure you keep toxic materials on a high shelf in your shed or garage.

GARAGE DOOR

Make sure that the child-protection auto-reverse setting is operating properly. Keep garage doors closed to keep little ones out.

CARS

Keep your vehicle doors locked so your little one can't play race-car driver.

GARDEN EQUIPMENT

Lawn mowers, other electrical yard equipment, and even small trowels and rakes can be dangerous if children get their hands on them. Store these in a locked shed.

BBQ | EQUIPMENT

Keep sharp edges out of reach, like BBQ accessories. Make sure the BBQ is turned off and always monitor it when in use to prevent children from getting too close.

CHOKING HAZARDS

Literally everything seems to want to go directly into a baby's mouth. So identifying and removing objects that are potential choking hazards is important, as is knowledge of infant CPR.

QUICK TIP
Among the top choking hazards for kids are **hot dogs** and **grapes**.

CHOKING:

Choking happens when objects, usually food or toys, get stuck in the airway and block one's ability to breathe. If airflow in and out of the lungs is blocked, it can deprive the brain of oxygen and is a life-threatening emergency.

FOODS THAT CAN BE CHOKING HAZARDS

 GRAPES: Grapes should be cut lengthwise and quartered without their skin.

 HARD CANDIES: Many candies, including hard candy, can cause choking.

 NUTS & SEEDS: These are hazards for young children largely due to their inability to grind food.

 PEANUT BUTTER: Globs of peanut butter can be a choking hazard.

 HOT DOGS: If you give hot dogs to children, it is safest to cut them lengthwise and in small pieces.

 TAFFY: Dangerous because it can mold and conform to block a child's airway.

 POPCORN: Popcorn is a risk due to a young child's inability to chew well.

 GUM: Gum can block a child's airway.

 RAW FRUITS: Small fruits may be dangerous if not chewed properly.

 RAW VEGETABLES: Large pieces of hard vegetables become a choking hazard if not chewed.

 WATERMELON: Watermelon seeds can be a hazard.

 MEAT & CHEESE: Meats and cheeses should be cut into small pieces.

TIPS ON FOOD AND CHOKING

- Encourage kids to sit when eating and to chew thoroughly.

- Teach children to chew and swallow their food before talking or laughing.

- Be vigilant during adult parties. Clean up promptly and check the floor for dropped foods that can cause choking.

- Never let kids with food run, play, or ride in the car unsupervised.

- Don't give any hard, smooth foods to kids younger than four.

COMMON HOUSEHOLD CHOKING HAZARDS

SMALL TOYS: Small toys or toys with small parts that can break off or come apart, as well as small doll accessories.

COINS: Any change is a potential choking hazard.

BALLOONS: Latex balloons with the air let out of them are dangerous.

PEN CAPS: Caps from markers and pens can be a real problem.

OFFICE SUPPLIES: Paper clips, tacks, etc. can be hazards.

PLASTIC CAPS: Plastic bottle caps are major choking hazards.

BATTERIES: Small-sized batteries can be dangerous.

NAILS: Nails, bolts, and screws are hazards.

MARBLES: Marbles and small round toys pose a threat.

BROKEN CRAYONS: Broken crayons and chalk can be dangerous.

ERASERS: Individual erasers or those broken off from pencils are problems.

JEWELRY: Small earrings, rings, necklaces, etc. can be dangerous.

CHOKING HAZARDS

In the United States, the Child Safety Protection Act requires warning labels on packaging for toys containing small parts—this is called the small-parts warning, which indicates a potential choking hazard.

KEEP AN EYE ON THEM

One thing that blew my mind was the ability of our babies to find any small piece of random stuff on the floor. It never failed that my son or daughter would find a leaf or some piece of paper or plastic. My point is that you really have to be careful because no matter how clean you keep your home, babies seem to have some special radar for finding potentially dangerous stuff.

PREVENTION & TIPS

- Never leave small children unattended while they are eating.
- Make sure children are sitting down while they are eating.
- Keep small objects out of the reach of children.
- Make sure meals and snack times are calm and unhurried.
- Don't allow children to eat when walking, riding in a car, or playing.
- Cut foods into small pieces and remove seeds and pits.
- Avoid toys with small parts.
- Give children sticky foods only in small amounts.
- Encourage kids to chew their food properly.
- Educate your caregivers about choking hazards.
- Know your emergency resources and contact information.
- Learn lifesaving techniques like child CPR and the Heimlich maneuver.

1.25 INCHES

QUICK TIP

Take a simple paper towel roll or toilet paper roll, and if a toy or object can pass through it, it is a potential choking hazard for your baby.

DOGS & BABY

Pets are a wonderful thing for kids and can be an amazing part of a child's life, but pets can also become jealous if they are no longer the center of your attention. By planning ahead and taking the right steps, your baby's homecoming will not throw your household into chaos.

TIPS FOR INTRODUCING BABIES TO DOGS

A TRAINER

If your dog is problematic before your baby arrives, consider enrolling him in obedience classes or hiring a trainer to come to your home.

MAKE CHANGES TO YOUR DOG'S ROUTINES EARLY

It's important not to completely change your dogs' routine: when you walk them, where they sleep, when they eat, etc., so they don't associate the change with the baby. If you know there will be changes in the dog's routine, then make those changes several months before baby comes home.

PLAY RECORDING OF BABY SOUNDS

Babies can be loud and noisy, which can freak out some dogs. Help your dog become accustomed to the sounds of a baby by playing recorded baby sounds.

LET YOUR DOG GET FAMILIAR WITH BABY SMELLS

Introduce some of the scents of babies, like soap or diapers, ahead of time.

A SPACE FOR FIDO/SAFETY ZONE

If you know in what areas of the house the baby will be crawling, put up gates early to contain those areas. This creates a safety zone outside those areas for pets—when you need to contain pets, you put them outside the gated areas. When baby starts walking and the pets want to escape the little monster, they have a place to retreat to.

GREETING THE DOGS

When home from the hospital, don't bring the baby in right away. First go in and show your dog lots of love. Then, when you bring in the baby, the dog will be calmer and not jump up or fight for attention.

LET DOGS GRADUALLY GET USED TO BABY

Don't rush to present baby to pets. Give your pets time to get used to the smells and sights of your new baby. Just go about your normal business, and let everyone get into a routine.

INTRODUCING THE BABY

When introducing your pets to baby, do so in a controlled manner. First, give the dog a lot of love and attention, and then allow the dog to approach you and baby. I suggest putting your dog on a leash to start with to ensure you have control, and let the dog come closer to see and smell the baby. Don't allow the dog to get in baby's face and never scold the dog for coming close to baby.

NORMAL INTERACTION

Once your dog is used to the smells and sounds of baby, you can proceed to off leash. When interacting, always keep baby elevated and away from the dog. The baby should never be left unsupervised with the dog.

WHOSE TOY IS IT?

If the dog takes one of the baby's toys, never scold the dog or grab away the toy. Instead, have extra dog toys on hand, and if the dog gets a baby toy, just replace it with a dog toy.

DOGGY KISSES

Every once in a while, your dog will try and sneak in a kiss. Don't overreact, but you might want to shy away from it. It's not likely that the dog will pass on germs to your baby, but it's not worth the risk while baby is so young.

DOGS & BABY

CRAWLING BABIES

With baby crawling at the dog's level, the dog will be curious. Always be very careful not to let your dogs step on, scratch, or roll onto the baby. Never leave a baby unsupervised with pets.

TODDLERS ARE ROUGH

Toddlers will be interested in your pets, too, but they have to learn how to interact with them in a gentle way. At first, they are naturally rough. You'll need to carefully prevent kids from stepping on the dog and pulling the dog's hair or tail, as this can result in snapping and growling.

Take the kids' hands and show them the proper way to pet or interact with the dog. A lot of verbal reinforcement, "Gentle, gentle, gentle," is necessary.

DOGS AND THE NURSERY

In general, keep dogs out of the baby's room—dogs don't need to be in there. Install a baby gate in the nursery, or shut the door. This is especially necessary if the pets are curious and attempt to jump up on the crib or the changing table.

DOGS AND FEEDING TIME

Here's something you can do to help dogs think of baby as a positive: when the child is in the high chair and food hits the floor, let it be a freebie for the dog. With little ones, food dropping on the floor is part of any meal, and your pets will soon look forward to the baby's mealtime as much as their own.

CAUTION

Safety is ultimately the goal. We want pets and kids to be safe and well-adjusted together. It's wise to always supervise and manage the interactions of young children and household pets. Realize that as good-natured as a dog can be, accidents do happen, and it's wise to err on the side of caution.

CLEANING PRODUCTS

Many common household cleaning products can be harmful to baby, both before and after birth. You should limit exposure to these chemicals and take protective measures when you use them.

AVOID PRODUCTS THAT CONTAIN:

Chlorine	Phthalates	Nonylphenol	1,4-Dioxane
Formaldehyde	Bisphenol	Ethoxylate	Fluoride
Solvents	Methoxychlor	Cresol	Hydrochloric acid
Ammonia	Phenol		
Sodium acid sulfate	Sodium hypochlorite		

QUICK TIP

All household cleaning products should be placed in locked cabinets on high shelves, out of reach of children.

POISON CONTROL

For emergencies, call 1-800-222-1222.

DIY HOUSEHOLD CLEANERS

VINEGAR AND WATER

The acidity in vinegar can cut through grease and help disinfect any surface. However, it's not ideal for stone as it can dull the surface.

1/3 cup distilled water

2/3 cup white vinegar

And a little bit of liquid soap

BAKING SODA

This nontoxic cleaning product is ideal for getting out tough stains on surfaces. Whether it's cleaning your ovens, showers, or toilets, baking soda can handle it all. Combine baking soda with hydrogen peroxide to scrub off any buildup, grime, or soap scum.

HYDROGEN PEROXIDE

Hydrogen peroxide can be used to clean lots of different things. It is like a bleach but better for the environment. It's a nice option if you need a deeper clean to remove stains, disinfect surfaces, or get rid of mold and mildew. You can also use it to whiten your laundry.

CASTILE SOAP

This is a soap made exclusively from vegetable oils, making it biodegradable and nontoxic. Don't combine it with any vinegar cleaning solutions because using both at the same time can leave a white film residue that's hard to get out.

DON'T WANT TO DIY?

There are more options on the market for nontoxic and environmentally friendly cleaning products today. Ideally, products should be petroleum-free, biodegradable, and phosphate-free.

There are also more products that are termed "safer options." Although such products are not 100 percent nontoxic or environmentally safe, they are a better alternative than their more toxic versions. Ultimately, it is up to you to decide what is best for you and your family.

So let
the adventures
begin!

OUT & ABOUT
GOING MOBILE WITH BABY

All the things you need to have and know to make venturing out with baby less stressful and a bit easier.

THE MUST-HAVES
FOR TRAVELING WITH BABY

DIAPER BAG

A diaper bag is a storage bag with many pockets and spaces big enough to carry everything needed to take care of your baby while you're away from home for short periods of time.

CAR SEAT

A child safety seat is designed specifically to protect children from injury during vehicle collisions. Look for models that have a five-point harness (two shoulder straps, two waist straps, and one strap between the legs) and padding around the head for side-impact protection. Ideally, It should be able to grow with your child and be compatible with the current car LATCH system.

STROLLER

A must-have travel system for transporting your kids. There are many different types of strollers; which you choose depends on your needs and budget.

PORTABLE CRIB OR PLAYPEN

A piece of furniture that can be folded down for transportation; it functions as a contained space for infants and young toddlers to prevent them from getting into trouble while the parent or guardian is occupied nearby.

CAR MIRROR

The mirror allows you to keep an eye on baby even though it is facing the back of the vehicle while you are driving. They should be made of shatterproof glass and be adjustable and easy to install.

DIGITAL DEVICE

Whether a phone, tablet, or computer, having a device to play age-appropriate content is a great way to keep kids occupied when you're traveling.

BACKPACK

It is very handy to have a backpack with lots of pockets for trips, especially when traveling by plane, when you need your hands to be free.

SUNSCREEN

Pick a broad-spectrum sunscreen with an SPF of at least 50. It should contain hypoallergenic ingredients like zinc oxide or titanium dioxide.

GET THE RIGHT STUFF!

Go to Simplestbaby.com for recommendations of the smartest baby products and essentials.

WHAT YOU NEED DIAPER BAG

CHECKLIST

- 3–4 diapers
- 1 bottle of milk
- 2 snacks
- 1 sippy cup of water
- 1 portable changing pad
- 1 pack of disposable wipes
- 2–3 plastic bags
- 1 diaper rash ointment
- 1 burping cloth
- 1 hand sanitizer
- 1 baby personal care kit
  (nail clipper, comb, emery board)
- 1 change of clothes for baby
- 1 hat for baby
- 2–3 baby toys
- 1 pacifier and 1 teether
- 1 bottle of sunscreen
- 1 blanket or swaddle
- 1 emergency information list
- 1 first aid kit
- 1 baby Tylenol or ibuprofen

IF BREASTFEEDING

- 1 nursing cover
- 2 breast pads

IN YOUR

Daddy Hack

It's helpful to keep your diaper bag prepacked and ready to go with everything but perishables. This is a real time-saver. Also having an extra change of clothes for you is a good idea.

GET THE RIGHT STUFF!
Go to Simplestbaby.com for recommendations of the smartest baby products and essentials.

STROLLERS
WHAT YOU NEED TO KNOW

One thing you will absolutely need is a stroller. There are many different types of strollers; here is the breakdown to help you find the one that works best for you.

TYPES OF STROLLERS

FULL-SIZE STROLLER

This is the heavy-duty workhorse of a stroller. It can weigh 16–30 lb. and often comes with many convenience and comfort features. It's usable from day one until your child is a toddler and usually has two smaller wheels in front, allowing for easier steering, and two larger wheels in back for stability.

LIGHTWEIGHT UMBRELLA STROLLER

A lightweight stroller that gets its name from its ability to fold up into a compact, travel-friendly size. Usually weighs 15 lb. or less. This is great for quick outings.

JOGGING STROLLER

Made to carry baby while you are running, walking, or hiking. It is typically made with superior suspension systems. It has three wheels, with the front being fixed, not swiveling. Hand brakes as well as foot brakes are common. It typically has oversized, air-filled tires. Many have adjustable handlebars, which can be put in several positions to make running or jogging more comfortable.

DOUBLE STROLLER

A stroller designed with two seats for twins or two young children who are close in age.

It comes in two types: tandem (where one child sits behind the other) or side by side.

CAR SEAT CARRIER STROLLER

This is a lightweight, frame device that is designed to carry a car seat and converts it into a stroller.

TRAVEL-SYSTEM STROLLER

This stroller system combines both a stroller and a car seat in one. They are specifically designed to work together. The infant car seat snaps onto the stroller frame and comes with a car-seat base.

GET THE RIGHT STUFF!
Go to Simplestbaby.com for recommendations of the smartest baby products and essentials.

TRAVELING BY CAR
ROAD-TRIP ESSENTIALS

Whether for a short or long road trip, here are some tips for avoiding potholes and keeping things running smoothly.

TIPS FOR SURVIVING A ROAD TRIP

PREP YOUR CAR

Make sure your vehicle is safe and ready ahead of time. Fill up the tank with gas, check the tire pressure, change the oil if needed, and pack all the gear you need ahead of time.

START SMALL

Make trips with young children short ones. As little ones grow, so do their attention spans, allowing them to sit for longer stretches of time in the car.

STOP FREQUENTLY

Determine rest stops before your trip. This way, you can pick stops that are entertaining to your kids. Be prepared to stop every couple of hours. You might even want to schedule your stops around baby's feedings.

SIT IN THE BACK

If you are traveling with another adult, it helps if one grown-up can take turns riding in the backseat for at least a portion of the trip.

PACK SNACKS

Pack bottles for babies during road trips and a cooler of treats, drinks, and snacks to eat along the way.

BRING TOYS & GAMES

Have a stock of toys and games that will entertain baby.

PACK EVERYTHING

Have a well-packed diaper bag with an extra change of clothes, extra diapers, drinks, sunblock, bug spray, medicines, food, water, shoes, blankets, and lots of wipes. Or have a well-packed baby caddy in your car.

KEEP IT CLOSE

Keep the essentials you'll need close to you: toys, bottles, sippy cups, pacifiers, snacks, etc. The worst thing is to have to dig around for them or stop the car.

CRANK UP THE TUNES

Music can be great for keeping kids content and entertained during a family road trip. Even better is to sing songs with the kids.

PROVIDE DIGITAL ENTERTAINMENT

Even if you don't allow your children to watch TV or videos at home, you may consider it for a road trip with a baby or toddler.

BRING EXTRA PLASTIC BAGS & CLOTHING

You never know when you'll need an extra change of clothes or a plastic bag for a soiled diaper or clothing.

HAVE A SLING OR FRONT CARRIER

You may need to be hands-free to help your other kids, so a sling is nice to have as you travel because you may not know if there will be stairs or hills that make it awkward to use a stroller.

CONSIDER NIGHT DRIVING

Consider driving at night when baby may be sleeping. You'll be able to drive for longer stretches without needing breaks.

KEEP YOUR COOL

Be patient with each other. Things inevitably will happen that will try your patience, but getting too frustrated will not make things any better for anyone.

PROVIDE WINDOW SHADES

Window shades to keep the sun off baby and help with naps can be really helpful.

THE CAR SEAT
A CAR ESSENTIAL

It is a requirement that you have a car seat installed in your car in order to leave the hospital with your baby. However, the laws governing car seats are set by each individual state, so you will need to check your specific state's requirements.

WHAT IS A CAR SEAT?

This is a seat that is designed specifically to protect children from injury or death during vehicle collisions.

TYPES OF CAR SEATS

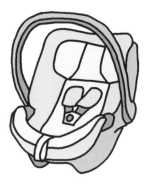

**INFANT CARRIER OR
INFANT CAR SEAT
(multiuse)**

This car seat functions as a travel system in that it latches into a base that stays in your car and can be snapped into specific strollers or stroller frames. It is intended to be used in rear-facing position only and is good from birth to about two years old. It is convenient because it doubles as a carrier. You can also purchase multiple bases to use in multiple cars.

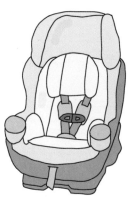

**CONVERTIBLE SEAT
(stays in car)**

This type of car seat grows with your child. It is used in a rear-facing position for baby and forward-facing as your child grows to a toddler. It uses different belting methods for the car's seat when forward-facing and the LATCH belt method when rear-facing. Some convert to booster seats as your child grows. These car seats cannot be used as carriers; they remain in the car.

WHAT TO LOOK FOR

When buying a car seat, there are several key things to consider and look for.

EASY TO CLEAN

SIDE-IMPACT PROTECTION
Look for extra foam or air pads on both sides of baby's head.

NEVER BUY A USED CAR SEAT.

EASILY ADJUSTABLE HARNESS STRAPS

5-POINT HARNESS:
two shoulder straps, two waist straps, and one strap between the legs that meet in the middle.

LATCH SYSTEM
Safety belting system that works with the latch system.

RIGHT SIZE
Read the label on the car seat to make sure the weight, height, and age limits of the car seat are right for your child.

GET THE RIGHT STUFF!

Go to Simplestbaby.com for recommendations of the smartest baby products and essentials.

THE LATCH SYSTEM
REAR-FACING CARSEAT BELTING

WHAT IS IT?

LATCH (Lower Anchors and Tethers for Children): It is a way to secure a child car seat to the vehicle using straps from the child car seat that connect to special metal anchors in the vehicle.

The LATCH system is required on car seats and in most vehicles manufactured on or after September 1, 2002.

WARNING

Directions on how to install your car seat with the LATCH system will be provided in the car seat instruction manual and/or will be printed on the side of the seat. Be sure to follow the instructions for your specific car seat for proper installation.

LATCH SYSTEM BELT HARDWARE
WHERE IT IS AND HOW IT WORKS

REAR-FACING CAR SEAT BELTING

The LATCH system hardware in your car is located between the rear seat cushion and the seat back. These metal hooks are the anchor points for the rear-facing car seat anchor belts.

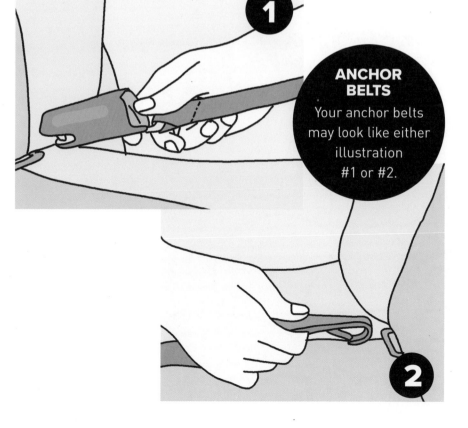

ANCHOR BELTS

Your anchor belts may look like either illustration #1 or #2.

FASTENING & TIGHTENING

Once anchor belts are attached to the anchor point, pull the belt to tighten it. It helps to put some of your weight on the seat as you tighten, for a snug fit. Once installed, the base or car seat should not move more than one inch side to side. If it moves more than that, it is not secure enough.

BREASTFEEDING IN PUBLIC

Breastfeeding in public is legal in all 50 states. Women have a right to breastfeed outside of their homes. Further, the Patient Protection and Affordable Care Act requires employers to provide reasonable time for breaks for nursing mothers.

QUICK TIP
Feed babies before they become fussy. When you get to your destination, scout out a comfortable place where you can breastfeed.

TIPS FOR BREASTFEEDING IN PUBLIC

PRACTICE, PRACTICE, PRACTICE

Before going out, try practicing at home in front of a mirror so you can see what you look like while breastfeeding. You can see if you are exposing your breast, so you will be able to make any adjustments if needed before feeding in public. This can also be helpful if you are using a nursing bra, as you can practice undoing it with one hand at home first.

PLAN AHEAD

It's a good idea to make a list of feeding-friendly locations ahead of time, so you know where you can feed—a place that is comfortable and semi-private. Make sure your diaper bag is packed with everything you might need for nursing: burp cloths, blankets, wipes, and water.

DRESS FOR SUCCESS

When it comes to what to wear when breastfeeding in public, there are lots of options. A few great choices: two-piece outfits, wrap-style dresses you can open from the front, and nursing tops or shirts that button from the bottom up, lift up, or pull to the side easily. You can also try a nursing cover-up or a simple shawl or poncho to use when breastfeeding.

CHOOSE THE RIGHT BRA

Stretchy sports-type bras or nursing bras might be better choices for easier access than a bra that closes in the back.

HAVE A RESPONSE READY

Be ready to have a response if someone confronts you. First, smile, stay positive and upbeat knowing that you have the right to breastfeed. If things escalate and you are asked to move or cover up, have a kind response prepared, especially if you are being careful to cover yourself and baby.

RESTAURANTS & BABY
SURVIVING EATING OUT WITH JUNIOR

Taking your baby to a restaurant can be extremely stressful, especially your first time. Will baby have a meltdown, will baby sit still, will others think you're a bad parent, and is it even worth doing?

TIPS FOR SURVIVING DINING OUT

MAKE A RESERVATION

Waiting in line for a table with fussy kids is not a pleasure.

DINE EARLY

Dining early can reduce the crowd size and create less chance of a meltdown in front of a crowd.

BLOW OFF A LITTLE STEAM

Before you go out, it's helpful if the kids are not worked up.

BRING SNACKS

Having snacks or some food ready in case you have to wait for the food to be served can be helpful.

MUNCH ON BREAD

A well-timed piece of bread can be a big help in filling the time before the food arrives.

ORDER QUICKLY

The sooner you can place your order, the better, even if you order only an appetizer.

GET THE CHECK EARLY

While you are still eating, it's a good idea to ask for the check so that baby is not waiting.

BRING YOUR DIAPER BAG

Having your diaper bag well stocked and handy is very important.

CHOOSE THE RIGHT TABLE

Being smart about where you sit is helpful: sit close to the exit or take a corner table away from most people. Be sure that the table is large enough to give you room for everything you will need.

CHOOSE THE RIGHT RESTAURANT

Make sure that you have chosen a restaurant that is kid-friendly. A casual restaurant is a better choice than a Michelin-starred restaurant.

BE QUICK ABOUT IT

Don't linger: your little angel can change to a little devil in a heartbeat, so expecting to hang out and enjoy the scene is not in the cards.

HAVE A VIDEO READY

Whatever anyone says about it, digital or video content can be a real lifesaver when eating out with kids.

TIP WELL

Tip your waiter well, especially if the kids have made a mess of the table, the chairs, the floor, and anywhere close to them.

Daddy Hack

More than likely, your first ventures out will be challenging. Keep them short, and be prepared to leave if things get out of hand. Think of the experience as training for you and baby.

TRAVELING BY PLANE
EVERYTHING YOU WILL NEED TO KNOW

Afraid of being that parent—the one everyone hates to see—a parent with a baby or toddler? You are not alone; we all have those fears. Flying with babies and kids is hard! There is no such thing as a stress-free flying experience. Here are some ideas and things you need to know to have a smoother flight.

RESTRICTIONS

Many airlines have restrictions on how old babies must be before they can fly. Generally speaking, the major airlines require a baby be at least two to eight days old before traveling. Those that do permit babies under seven days old to fly generally ask for a medical release or physician's note stating that the baby is cleared to fly. Check with the airline to confirm its specific requirements.

LONG FLIGHTS

On a longer or international flight, you may wish to request a seat assignment with a bassinet if your baby will still fit into a bassinet.

Daddy Hack

I can't stress enough the importance of planning ahead for traveling. Trust me, things will go sideways and you will be thankful that you thought and prepared ahead of time.

TIPS FOR SURVIVING FLYING WITH BABY

CARRY-ON TRAVEL BAG FOR BABY

Using a carry-on backpack-style diaper bag will keep your hands free because you will need them. Make sure it contains all the essentials.

PLAN FOR A CAR SEAT

Babies and infants must be in a car seat while you are traveling to and from the airport. There are several ways to deal with having a car seat.

1. Bring your car seat for the taxi or rental car.
2. Contact the car rental agency and see if they can provide one.

If you bring your car seat on the plane, you will have to make sure it's an FAA-approved car seat. You also should familiarize yourself with how to install the car seat in a plane, which you can find in your car seat manual.

BRING A STROLLER

Bring a collapsible stroller that is lightweight or one that is made to work with a car seat. Having a stroller to move baby around is a must. Carrying just a small baby over time will wear out even the strongest arms.

BOOK A DIRECT FLIGHT

Keep connecting flights to a minimum. If you have several flights to get to your destination, give yourself plenty of time between flights. Running to catch a flight is a pain on your own but incredibly worse with kids in tow.

MAKE A PIT STOP

Before boarding the flight, make one last trip to the restroom.

DISINFECT EVERYTHING

You will want to bring disinfectant wipes and run them over **everything** your little one might touch on the plane—seat, seat belt, tray table, etc.

GIVE YOURSELF TIME

Give yourself **plenty** of time so you're not rushed. Arrive at the airport extra early so you can check in, get through security, and do everything you need to without being stressed for time.

BRING PLASTIC BAGS

Have some ziplock plastic bags just in case things get messy and you need to put dirty or soiled clothing or items in your bag.

TRAVELING BY PLANE

MORE TIPS FOR FLYING WITH BABY

USE THE PRE-BOARD

Boarding ahead of the crowd is very, very helpful. If you are flying with a partner, see if he or she can board first and stow the luggage, wipe down everything, and get things ready. When you board, everything will be ready and baby has not been sitting for half an hour waiting for everyone else to board.

BUY A SEAT FOR YOUR CHILD

Having a seat for your baby is nice, especially the older your baby is. It gives you and the family more room to spread out.

PACK JUST RIGHT

Bring twice as much as you think you will need on the plane of formula, diapers, baby food, and snacks. Don't overpack on all the other stuff.

CHECK THE GEAR AT THE GATE

Most airlines allow parents to gate-check strollers and car seats at no charge. Simply request gate-check tags from the attendant at the gate.

BRING A PORTABLE CRIB | PLAYPEN

A safe place for your baby to sleep or play—either you can bring yours or ship it ahead to lighten the load and avoid baggage fees.

DRESS BABY IN COMFORTABLE LAYERS

The temperature in a plane can change from boiling hot to downright chilly. Choose attire for baby that is cozy and easy to change. Wearing layers is also helpful for breastfeeding moms.

PACK BABY MEDICATION

Pack prescription and over-the-counter medicine you may need for baby.

PROTECT THE EARS

Sucking or chewing helps ease potential ear pain caused by pressure changes in the plane. Give your baby a bottle, sippy cup, or pacifier during takeoff and landing.

HAVE AN IPAD

Having entertaining content preloaded and ready is extremely helpful. Check ahead of time whether the particular airline has an entertainment app that needs to be loaded. Don't assume that you will have Wi-Fi on the plane.

Daddy Hack

Using a backpack with lots of pockets in place of a traditional diaper bag will help keep your hands free for everything else that is going to come up, and it will.

PACK EARLY

Start preparing to pack a few days before you travel. Keep a running list of things to take, or lay out items on a table or dresser.

GET PAPERWORK IN ORDER

Have your baby's travel-related paperwork with you when you fly, especially if your baby has a different last name, appears to be of a different race, or if you are an LGBTQ family. This could be a birth certificate, passport, or documentation from the hospital and/or physician's office.

HAVE A CHANGE OF CLOTHES

Pack an extra change of clothing in your carry-on for you and your baby in case an unfortunate throw-up happens mid-flight.

GO TSA PRECHECK

Absolutely worth doing, having TSA PreCheck or Global Entry helps streamline the process. It was a blessing for us.

PREP FOR A BOTTLE

Have your formula powder already measured out in individual plastic bags and get a bottle or two of water while in the airport for mixing.

HANDS-FREE

Consider carrying the baby in a child carrier through the airport; it will help keep those all-important hands free.

CARRY-ON TRAVEL BAG

A diaper bag is for those short out-and-about trips, like shopping or going to the park, but we recommend using a backpack for air travel. You will also need to pack it differently. Here is the perfect list of items to pack in your baby backpack.

BACKPACK

Invest in a good backpack over your regular diaper bag as it makes carrying all the things for traveling far easier. Especially when flying, you'll need to keep your hands as free as possible to deal with the various things that will come up.

ESSENTIALS FOR AN INFANT CARRY-ON BAG

- Diapers (always pack more than you think you might need)
- Baby wipes (lots of wipes)
- Disinfecting wipes (to wipe down and disinfect almost everything)
- Changing pads or pee pads
- Blanket
- Plastic bags for unfortunate mishaps
- Burp cloth
- Diaper rash cream
- Teether
- Disinfecting hand gel
- Tissues
- Ear-pressure protectors or something to get baby swallowing
- Sippy cup
- Toys and books
- Your child's favorite plush
- Change of clothing for baby and you (just in case)
- Formula (have powder premeasured in separate plastic bags)
- Pain medicine (just in case)
- Anti-gas medicine (depends on your baby)
- iPad (preloaded) and headphones, depending on the child's age
- Snacks (depending on your child's age)
- Bib
- Lightweight plastic feeding utensils
- Passports
- Travel pillow
- Pacifier

THINGS TO PACK IN YOUR CHECKED ITEMS

- Additional clothing for you
- Child's shampoo
- Child's toothbrush and toothpaste
- First aid care items
- Bathing suit and swim diapers
- Jars of baby food
- Socket protectors (or painter's tape)
- Portable crib or playpen
- Car seats
- Comb, brush, and nail clippers
- Children's sunscreen
- Breast pump

A PASSPORT FOR BABY
WHAT TO KNOW AND DO

PROVIDE TWO PASSPORT PHOTOS AND PAY FEES

- Provide two color photos of the newborn baby.
- The photos must be identical and 2 x 2 inches in size.
- The photos must be recent.
- The photo must have the baby's full face, front view, with a plain white background.
- No one else should be present in the photograph.
- If the baby is unable to sit upright, the picture may be taken with the baby lying down on a white surface.

PROCESSING TIME

The entire processing time for applying for a passport for a newborn or child takes four to six weeks. However, expedited processing is available for an additional fee. Expedited service takes three weeks for processing or only eight business days if expedited at the agency. The expedited service fee is $60 USD.

EVIDENCE OF U.S. CITIZENSHIP (OPTIONS)

- Certified birth certificate issued by the city, county, or state
- Consular report of American birth abroad
- Previously issued U.S. passport
- Naturalization certificate
- Certificate of citizenship

SHOW EVIDENCE OF RELATIONSHIP

You will have to prove that you are the newborn baby's parents. All documents must be submitted in original. These will serve as evidence:

- Certified birth certificate with both parents' names.
- If the child was born abroad, you should submit the following:
  - Child's certified Foreign Birth Certificate with names of both parents
  - Child's Report of Birth Abroad with names of both parents

Formal or informal English translation must be submitted with all foreign documents.

- If the child is adopted, submit an adoption decree with the parents' names.
- If you are guardian to a newborn baby, you should submit the following:
  - Court order establishing custody
  - Court order establishing guardianship
  - Identification documents for parents

For more information go to:

https://travel.state.gov/content/travel/en/passports/need-passport/under-16.html

A healthy baby
is a happy baby.

HEALTH
KEEPING BABY HEALTHY & HAPPY

Health issues will arise with your new baby. We have included some of the more common things you may have to deal with and other things I wish someone had told me about.

THE MUST-HAVES

FOR COMMON BABY HEALTH ISSUES

DIGITAL THERMOMETER

You may need a couple of different thermometers. For babies three months or younger, a rectal digital thermometer is recommended. As baby gets older, closer to twelve months, you might consider a tympanic (ear) thermometer or infrared (IR) laser thermometer.

NOSE-CLEANING DEVICE

When your little one gets a stuffy nose, this device allows you to remove the mucus from baby's nose, helping to make it easier for baby to breathe.

SALINE MIST

A saline solution to moisten nasal sinuses and help to thin mucus makes it easier to remove mucus with a nose-cleaning device.

TOPICAL ANTIBIOTIC

These medications are antibacterial agents used to prevent infection of burns, minor cuts, and wounds.

PAIN-RELIEF MEDICINE

These medicines are used to relieve pain and fever. Your doctor can tell you about proper dosing of acetaminophen (Tylenol and others) or ibuprofen (Advil, Motrin, and others) for your baby.

TEETHER

Baby teethers are used to soothe babies' gums when their teeth start coming in, at around four to ten months of age. Look for teething toys that are durable, BPA-free, easy for your child to hold, and safe to chew on.

GAS-RELIEF DROPS

These products are used to relieve symptoms of extra gas caused by swallowing air or reactions to certain foods and infant formulas.

GRIPE WATER

Gripe water is a natural combination of herbs like ginger, fennel, chamomile, and cinnamon, which help ease stomach discomfort caused by excess gas in the stomach.

PROBIOTIC DROPS

Baby probiotic drops are a daily liquid probiotic supplement you can use from birth. They help maintain the balance of bacteria in the intestines that help ease gas, constipation, and colic.

STERILE GAUZE PADS

Gauze is a light, thin, loosely woven fabric commonly made of cotton or a synthetic fiber. Sterile pads are used for many medical purposes, especially to treat small-to-medium cuts, burns, and scrapes.

HUMIDIFIER

A cool-mist vaporizer or humidifier adds moisture to the air and can help your baby breathe easier when baby is congested.

GET THE RIGHT STUFF!
Go to Simplestbaby.com for recommendations of the smartest baby products and essentials.

IMMUNIZATION
SCHEDULE

Vaccinations are critically important to the health of a baby. The CDC and AAP recommend having your children vaccinated to protect them and avoid the spread of preventable diseases. Vaccinations will be a part of your normal visits to your doctor. Below is the recommended immunization schedule from the CDC, covering birth to one year of age. Keeping track of baby's vaccinations is simple with our checklist.

LIST OF RECOMMENDED VACCINES | WHEN GIVEN

Keep in mind that some of these vaccines may be part of a combination vaccine

BIRTH

DATE

_____ ☐ 1ST DOSE OF HEPATITIS B

2 MONTHS

DATE

_____ ☐ 1ST DOSE PCV13 (PNEUMOCOCCAL)

_____ ☐ 1ST DOSE DTaP (DIPHTHERIA, TETANUS, and PERTUSSIS)

_____ ☐ 1ST DOSE HIB (HAEMOPHILUS INFLUENZAE)

_____ ☐ 1ST DOSE IPV (POLIO)

_____ ☐ 2ND DOSE HEPATITIS B

_____ ☐ 1ST DOSE ROTAVIRUS

QUICK TIP

If you have concerns about giving too many vaccinations at one time, you can ask to have them spread out.

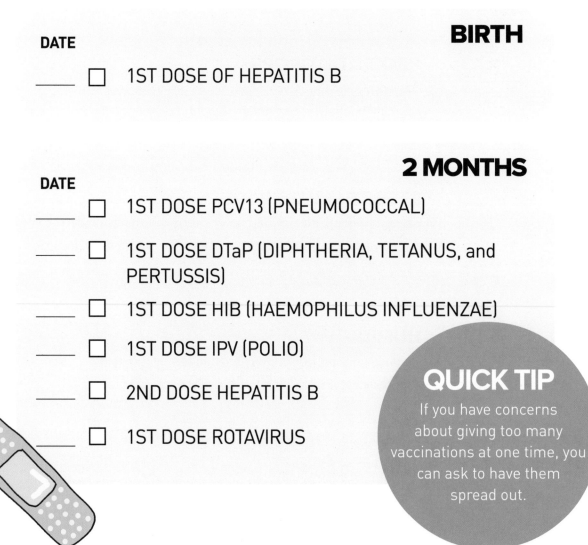

4 MONTHS

DATE

_____ ☐ 2ND DOSE PCV13 (PNEUMOCOCCAL)

_____ ☐ 2ND DOSE DTaP (DIPHTHERIA, TETANUS, and PERTUSSIS)

_____ ☐ 2ND DOSE IPV (POLIO)

_____ ☐ 2ND DOSE HIB (HAEMOPHILUS INFLUENZAE)

_____ ☐ 2ND DOSE ROTAVIRUS

6 MONTHS

DATE

_____ ☐ 3RD DOSE PCV13 (PNEUMOCOCCAL)

_____ ☐ 3RD DOSE DTaP (DIPHTHERIA, TETANUS, and PERTUSSIS)

_____ ☐ 3RD DOSE IPV (POLIO)

_____ ☐ 3RD DOSE HIB (HAEMOPHILUS INFLUENZAE)

_____ ☐ 3RD DOSE ROTAVIRUS

_____ ☐ 3RD DOSE OF HEPATITIS B

_____ ☐ FLU VACCINE

12 MONTHS

DATE

_____ ☐ MEASLES, MUMPS, and RUBELLA (MMR)

_____ ☐ CHICKENPOX (VARICELLA)

TEETHING

Teething is the term used to describe the process by which an infant's first teeth begin to come in. Although when babies get their teeth varies, babies usually begin to get their first teeth around six to eight months in the lower front.

SIGNS OF TEETHING

- Drooling
- Chewing on objects
- Irritability, fussiness, and crying
- Sore or tender gums
- Low-grade fever

- Disrupted sleep
- Swelling or inflammation of the gums
- Rash around the mouth
- Cheek rubbing and ear pulling

TIPS FOR SOOTHING SORE GUMS

MASSAGE GUMS:
Use a clean finger to rub your baby's gums. The pressure can help ease discomfort.

KEEP IT COOL:
A cold rubber spoon or chilled teething ring can be soothing for baby's gums. Don't give your baby a frozen teething ring as it might crack. Make sure the toy or teething ring is age appropriate, BPA-free, and nontoxic.

DRY THE DROOL:
Lots of drool is part of teething. To prevent skin irritation, keep a clean cloth handy to dry your baby's chin.

PAIN RELIEF:
Try an over-the-counter remedy. If your baby is especially cranky, acetaminophen (Tylenol and others) or ibuprofen (Advil, Children's Motrin, and others) might help. With all medications, check with your pediatrician first.

BABY TEETH ERUPTION CHART

UPPER TEETH

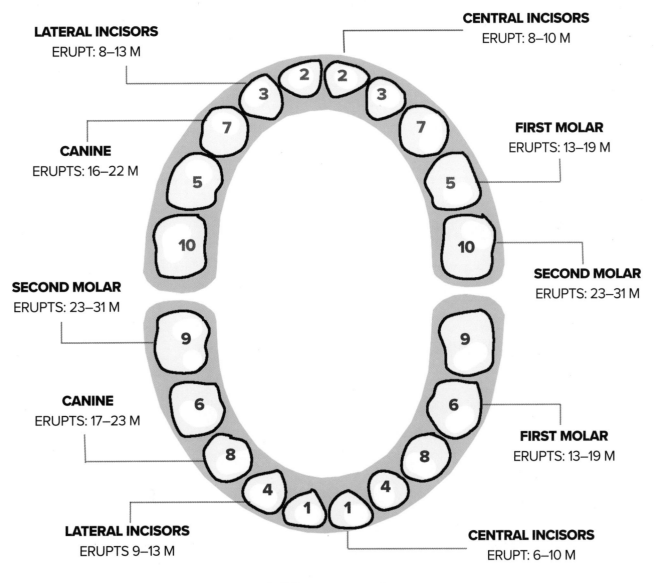

CENTRAL INCISORS
ERUPT: 8–10 M

LATERAL INCISORS
ERUPT: 8–13 M

CANINE
ERUPTS: 16–22 M

FIRST MOLAR
ERUPTS: 13–19 M

SECOND MOLAR
ERUPTS: 23–31 M

SECOND MOLAR
ERUPTS: 23–31 M

CANINE
ERUPTS: 17–23 M

FIRST MOLAR
ERUPTS: 13–19 M

LATERAL INCISORS
ERUPTS 9–13 M

CENTRAL INCISORS
ERUPT: 6–10 M

LOWER TEETH

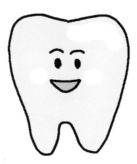

The chart is labeled 1 to 10: 1 being the first teeth that typically come in and 10 the last.

- The bottom front two teeth usually appear first around 6–10 months.
- The top front two teeth appear around 8–10 months.
- A complete set of 20 baby teeth erupt by 30 months of age.

JAUNDICE
MY BABY IS YELLOW!

WHAT IS IT?

Newborn jaundice is the yellowing of a baby's skin and eyes. It is very common and occurs when a baby has a buildup of bilirubin in their bloodstream. Bilirubin is a yellow pigment produced by the normal breakdown of red blood cells. It is more often found in babies who are born prematurely, before 38 weeks.

HOW IS IT DETECTED?

Your baby is usually examined for any signs of jaundice while at the hospital and by your pediatric doctor during checkups.

CAUSES OF JAUNDICE

- Baby is not getting enough breast milk or has formula due to feeding difficulties.

- Baby experienced bruising at birth or has internal bleeding.

- Baby has liver problems.

- Baby has a blood infection.

- Baby has an enzyme deficiency.

- Baby has an abnormality in red blood cells.

- Baby's blood is not compatible with the mother's.

The information provided is not a substitute for professional medical advice, diagnosis, or treatment. Always consult your pediatrician or health-care provider to ensure that a treatment is right for you and your child.

JAUNDICE TREATMENT

MILD-TO-MODERATE JAUNDICE

Newborn jaundice typically goes away on its own as a baby's liver matures and rids the body of bilirubin. Frequent feeding can help clear bilirubin levels from baby's system. Mild cases usually disappear within two to three weeks.

SEVERE JAUNDICE

Severe cases may require phototherapy, which is a common treatment that uses light to break down bilirubin in the baby's body. The baby will be placed under a blue spectrum light while wearing only a diaper and protective eye wear. A fibre-optic blanket may be placed underneath the baby.

VERY SEVERE JAUNDICE

If a baby has very severe jaundice, there's a risk of bilirubin passing into the brain. This can be very serious as bilirubin is toxic and can result in brain damage, cerebral palsy, and deafness.

Prompt treatment and a transfusion, where baby receives blood from a donor or a blood bank to replace baby's damaged blood with healthy red blood cells, may be necessary.

CRADLE CAP

WHAT IS IT?

Cradle cap is a common and harmless skin condition that causes crusty or oily white or yellow scales on a baby's scalp. These thick white or yellow scales are not painful, itchy, or contagious. Cradle cap usually clears up on its own in a few weeks or months.

COMMON SIGNS

- Patchy scales or crusts on the scalp
- Skin covered with flaky white or yellow scales
- Possible mild redness

CAUSES

The cause of cradle cap is unknown. One factor may be hormones that pass from the mother to the baby before birth. These hormones can cause too much production of oil in the oil glands and hair follicles.

TREATMENT

Shampoo your baby's hair with a mild, fragrance-free, hypoallergenic shampoo. Don't pick at the flakes; use a soft brush to gently remove the flakes.

The information provided is not a substitute for professional medical advice, diagnosis, or treatment. Always consult your pediatrician or health-care provider to ensure that a treatment is right for you and your child.

BABY ACNE

It may look like your baby is going through puberty with a breakout of pimples, but he is not; it's baby acne.

WHAT IS IT?

Baby acne is a skin condition that results in small red pimples that occur anywhere on the face but usually on the cheeks, nose, and forehead. Typically beginning at two to three weeks after birth, baby acne is common and temporary. There's little you can do to prevent it, and it usually clears up on its own without scarring.

CAUSES

The exact cause is not clear, but it's believed to be a result of maternal hormones still circulating in your baby's bloodstream. These hormones stimulate baby's oil-producing glands, causing pimples on the chin, forehead, eyelids, and cheeks (and sometimes the head, neck, back, and upper chest).

TREATMENT

Don't squeeze pimples.

Clean and dry
Keep your baby's face clean by washing every day with warm water or hypoallergenic soap; pat dry.

Breast milk
Breast milk is nature's wonder remedy and can be applied to the affected area to help ease the condition due to its antimicrobial properties.

Medicated creams
For stubborn cases, a medicated cream may be prescribed.

BABY ECZEMA
FLAKE OFF

Seeing your baby with red blotches and itchy, dry skin can be upsetting, but it is common and treatable.

WHAT IS IT?

Atopic dermatitis, or eczema, usually appears as red, crusty rough patches on the skin. Children typically grow out of it.

CAUSES

- Family history of the condition
- Skin barrier problem, allowing moisture out and germs in
- Body producing too few fatty cells, causing water loss from the skin

Things that aggravate the condition

- Scratchy clothing, fragrances, and soaps
- Low humidity | dry air
- Stress
- Heat and sweat
- Allergies; having an allergic reaction to certain food proteins

SYMPTOMS:

- Dry, flaky skin, typically on the cheeks, joints, arms, and legs
- Red itchy patches
- Rubbing cheeks or body on surfaces to get rid of the itch

TREATMENT & PREVENTION:

WARM BATH & MOISTURIZE

Bathing your baby daily can help to hydrate the skin, but you will want to keep the bath short, around ten to fifteen minutes. Pat dry, leaving a little moisture on the skin, and then apply moisturizer.

CREAMS & OINTMENTS

Use a fragrance-free moisturizer with ceramides. Petroleum jelly and Albolene can help the skin retain moisture. You should moisturize the affected areas several times a day. Depending on the severity, a topical anti-inflammatory or steroid cream may be prescribed.

HYPOALLERGENIC LAUNDRY DETERGENT

Use laundry detergents that are fragrance-free and hypoallergenic. Wash all clothing before wearing it. Do not use dryer sheets.

SOAP USAGE

Limit the use of soaps when washing or bathing baby, and always use fragrance-free soaps.

DRESS APPROPRIATELY

Dress baby in loose, comfortable clothing that breathes easily.

HONEY CRUSTING

If affected areas have a honey-colored crust over broken skin, contact your pediatrician, as it may indicate an infection.

The information provided is not a substitute for professional medical advice, diagnosis, or treatment. Always consult your pediatrician or health-care provider to ensure that a treatment is right for you and your child.

ERYTHEMA TOXICUM

Also called toxic erythema or newborn rash

WHAT IS IT?

Erythema Toxicum is a common condition affecting half of all full-term newborns. It usually appears as a rash with pus-filled blemishes soon after birth and clears up on its own in a few weeks.

HOW IS IT DETECTED?

It appears as a blotchy, red rash with small bumps that can be filled with a pus-like fluid on the baby's face, chest, arms, and legs.

CAUSES OF ERYTHEMA TOXICUM

The cause is unknown.

TREATMENT

No treatment is necessary, as the rash disappears on its own in 5–14 days. If it spreads, or rash becomes worse, consult your doctor.

- Avoid picking at or scrubbing the pimples.
- Wash baby's face with mild, fragrance-free soap and pat dry.
- Avoid using lotions or oils on baby's face.

The information provided is not a substitute for professional medical advice, diagnosis, or treatment. Always consult your pediatrician or health-care provider to ensure that a treatment is right for you and your child.

COLIC
KILL ME NOW!

There are few things worse than an inconsolable baby, and it's also one of the things that can drive parents to the edge of insanity!

WHAT IS IT?

COLIC: The general descriptive term for any healthy baby who has intense and excessive crying. Colic is definitely frustrating because the crying occurs for no explainable reason, and the baby appears to be inconsolable.

SYMPTOMS | SIGNS

- Prolonged, intense crying and screaming fits
- Crying lasting for hours for no apparent reasons
- Unable to be consoled
- Physical tightening of baby's legs, arms, and hands
- Extreme fussiness, even after crying has diminished
- Crying happening at predictable times in late afternoon and evening
- Flush reddening of face

CAUSES

The specific cause of colic is unknown. It may be the result of:

- An immature digestive system
- Lactose intolerance
- Hormones that cause discomfort and fussiness
- Oversensitivity to light, noise, or stimulation
- A developing nervous system

TREATMENT

As there is no clear understanding of the cause of colic, there is also not a clear treatment for it. Consult your pediatrician for the best solutions for your baby.

GASSY BABY?
PAINFUL FOR BABY & YOU

Gassiness in babies can be tough to handle and can cause considerable discomfort and crying for baby. Most of the time, it's due to baby's immature digestive system, swallowing too much air when eating, or being lactose intolerant.

As babies grow and mature, their bodies become better able to break down food and handle gas. In the meantime, here are some tips and advice to help let the air out.

8 TIPS FOR RELIEVING GASSINESS IN BABY

BICYCLE LEGS

Try working the gas out with bicycle legs. While seated, place your baby face up on a flat surface with baby's legs toward you. Then, slowly pump baby's legs in a somewhat circular motion, forward and backward, as if riding a bicycle.

THE RIGHT BOTTLE MATTERS

Use plastic or glass bottles that are free of BPA, BPS, and phthalates, and also have a venting anti-colic system designed to minimize air bubbles and help with reflux. This can be a real help. Make sure they are dishwasher safe and have clear measurement markings.

FORMULA CHANGE-UP

If you think baby is experiencing colic, your baby could actually be having trouble digesting the formula you are using. Try using another formula that is made for sensitive babies. You might have to try several different variants until you find one that works for you. Consult your doctor on what formula might work best.

RE-BURPING

Try burping baby again. The baby might have some additional gas that needs to be released, and re-burping may do the trick.

GAS-RELIEF DROPS

This medication breaks up gas bubbles in the stomach, making it easier for baby to pass gas. These drops can be given to baby directly or put in the bottle of milk after it is warmed. Consult your pediatrician on use of all medications.

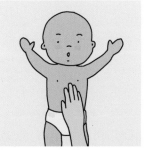

MASSAGE

With baby on her back, place your hand on her lower belly and abdomen and gently massage in a clockwise direction to help move gas bubbles along the intestinal tract. Avoid doing this if baby has just eaten.

WATCH WHAT YOU EAT

In some cases, gassiness may be a result of something in mom's diet, if mom is breastfeeding. Typically, babies are fine with whatever mom eats, however, if you notice gassiness when you eat certain foods, you might consider avoiding those.

LAP PAT

Lay your baby belly down on your lap. Support your baby's head and make sure it's higher than baby's chest. Gently pat your baby's back to help them release trapped gas.

BABY HAS A FEVER

One of the most stressful things for a parent is when your baby has a fever. A fever is a sign that your baby is fighting an illness. If your baby has a fever, in most cases, it means your baby has probably picked up a cold or other viral infection.

97°F–100.3°F **NORMAL TEMP**

. . . .

100.4°F **OR HIGHER** **FEVER**

THERMOMETERS

The American Academy of Pediatrics (AAP) recommends using digital rectal thermometers for babies. Never use a mercury thermometer to take a baby's temperature.

TYPES OF THERMOMETERS:

Rectal thermometers: Temperature taken by rectum. These are the most accurate thermometers and are recommended for taking the temperature of babies three months and younger.

Temporal thermometers: These are non-contact thermometers that use infrared light to take the temperature by forehead. They are the next most accurate after rectal and good for children three months and older.

Tympanic thermometers: Temperature taken by ear. These are quick and generally comfortable but not as accurate if done incorrectly.

Axillary thermometers: Temperature taken in armpit. This is one of the least accurate for taking a temperature.

Pacifier thermometers: Temperature taken by mouth. These work like a pacifier but also take temperature. As baby will grow out of it, it's not recommended.

WARNING: Never give your baby aspirin for a fever because of the risk of Reye's syndrome. Before giving any medication to your baby, be sure to consult your doctor.

WHAT TO DO IF BABY HAS A FEVER

- If your baby is three months or younger with a fever, call your doctor.
- If the baby is over three months, give acetaminophen (Tylenol) if recommended by your doctor.
- For babies who are older than six months, you can give them either children's Tylenol or ibuprofen (Advil or Motrin), as prescribed by the doctor.
- Apply a cool compress to baby's forehead.
- Give your baby enough fluids to avoid dehydration. Fluids should be breast milk, formula, an electrolyte solution, or water, depending on baby's age.
- Keep baby in a cool place 70°F–73°F.
- Remove extra clothing from baby.
- Give baby a sponge bath with lukewarm water.
- Dress your baby in light layers of clothes.

WHEN TO CALL THE DOCTOR

- Your baby is younger than three months and has a fever.
- Your baby is three to six months old and has a fever reaching 102°F (38.9°C).
- Your baby is lethargic and hard to awaken.
- Your baby has problems breathing.
- Your baby is very cranky or fussy.
- Your baby shows a lack of appetite or will not eat.
- Your baby has a rash.
- Your baby shows signs of being dehydrated.
- Your baby has a seizure or convulsions.

The information provided is not a substitute for professional medical advice, diagnosis, or treatment. Always consult your pediatrician or health-care provider to ensure that a treatment is right for you and your child.

BLOCKED TEAR DUCT

Ugh, what is this gunk in my baby's eyes? Don't panic: it's more than likely just a blocked tear duct, which is common in newborns.

WHAT IS IT?

Tears normally drain out of the eye through tear ducts, but some baby's tear ducts are not fully open at birth or are blocked. This causes a buildup and can become inflamed or irritated, producing a discharge that appears similar to that from an infection.

If the eye becomes very red, then you may be dealing with an infection. Blocked tear ducts generally clear up on their own without treatment.

CAUSES

- The tear duct has not opened completely.
- The tear duct is too narrow.
- An infection is present.
- Abnormal bone growth is blocking the tear duct path.

SYMPTOMS

- Watery eyes
- Slight redness and swollen eyelids
- Crusty discharge that causes eyelids to stick together
- Discharge from the eye that is yellow-green

The information provided is not a substitute for professional medical advice, diagnosis, or treatment. Always consult your pediatrician or health-care provider to ensure that a treatment is right for you and your child.

TIPS ON TREATING

CLEAN

Moisten a soft washcloth or cotton ball with warm water and gently clean the eye from the base of the nose outward. Do not wipe anything into the eye.

BREAST MILK

To help clear up the discharge and any possible infection, put a few drops of breast milk in the corner of the eye. Breast milk has natural infection-fighting properties that will help treat the problem.

CHAMOMILE TEA

If you don't have breast milk, you can brew some chamomile tea, let it cool, dip a cotton ball in the tea, and use it to wipe clean the discharge. You can also put a few drops of the tea in the corner of baby's eye. Chamomile has antibacterial properties. Consult your doctor.

EYE DROPS

Should the tear ducts become infected, your pediatrician or eye doctor will prescribe antibiotic drops or ointment for baby's eyes.

DUCT MASSAGE

You can apply gentle pressure to the tear duct and massage it to help it open. The duct is located between the lower eyelid and the nose. Consult your doctor on the proper massaging technique.

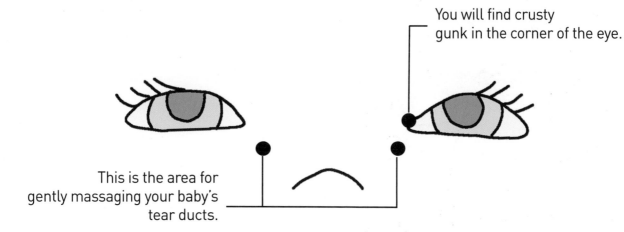

You will find crusty gunk in the corner of the eye.

This is the area for gently massaging your baby's tear ducts.

CONSTIPATION

Most of the time, it is normal for a baby to go a couple of days without a bowel movement. However, a baby may sometimes be constipated and need a little help.

WHAT IS IT?

Constipation is the term used to describe bowel movements that are difficult or happen less often than normal.

BABY CONSTIPATION

Normal baby bowel movements vary depending on the baby's age and what baby has eaten. Some may poop every day, others after several days. Straining while having a bowel movement is also normal with babies, as they have weak abdominal muscles.

Infant constipation often happens during the time when babies are having solids introduced into their diets. It can also happen if the formula you are using is too difficult for babies to digest. If you think your newborn is constipated, contact your doctor.

SYMPTOMS

- Hard, pellet-like poo
- Difficult and painful bowel movements with straining or crying
- Infrequent bowel movements
- Poop with blood in it or black poop
- Lack of appetite
- A hard belly

TIPS FOR TREATING CONSTIPATION

FORMULA

Speak with your pediatrician about changing the formula you are using to another variant that is easier for your baby to digest.

PROBIOTICS

Adding probiotic drops to baby's milk can help with baby's gut health and aid in bowel movements.

BABY FOOD

If your baby is old enough to eat solid food, try adding fruits and vegetables to your baby's diet. Try pureed peas, broccoli, carrots, peaches, plums, pears, or prunes—all have lots of fiber. Feed baby whole-grain cereals with barley or oat. If your baby is not old enough to eat solids, try introducing small amounts of fruit juices (prune, pear, cherry, or apple). Dilute these with water.

HYDRATION

Constipation can be the result of lack of hydration, although this is not common in infants as they are drinking lots of formula or breast milk. Speak to your pediatrician about giving baby a small amount of water. She may also suggest adding a small amount of prune juice to the water.

BICYCLE LEGS

This exercise might help stimulate a bowel movement. However, as babies may not be walking or even crawling yet, you're going to need to help them with the exercise. Gently move the baby's legs while baby is lying on her back to mimic the motion of riding a bicycle. Another common baby exercise is to very gently massage baby's tummy above the belly button in circular motions, moving away from the center of the belly.

A WARM BATH

Try giving baby a warm bath. It can relax your baby's muscles and help ease the passing of stool. Be prepared for a bit of poo in the tub.

The information provided is not a substitute for professional medical advice, diagnosis, or treatment. Always consult your pediatrician or health-care provider to ensure that a treatment is right for you and your child.

DIARRHEA

A baby with diarrhea is scary and worrisome to all parents. Here's what you need to know and do.

WHAT IS IT?

Bowel movements that are loose and have watery consistency and occur more often than normal.

Never give antidiarrheal medication to a baby.

BABY DIARRHEA

It's normal for baby poop to be soft and loose, especially during infancy. Baby diarrhea, however, is far more watery and slimy. Depending on what caused the diarrhea, the baby may also have an accompanying fever. Babies can become dehydrated in as little as a couple of days, which can be very dangerous to newborns.

CAUSES

VIRUSES

Rotavirus is a group of viruses that cause diarrhea in infants and children. Oral rotavirus vaccines have made this less common today.

DIET

A change in your baby's diet or the diet of the mother, if breastfeeding, can cause diarrhea. Diarrhea can also be caused by lactose intolerance or an allergic reaction to milk proteins.

BACTERIA

Escherichia coli, campylobacter, and salmonella are some of the causes of bacterial diarrhea.

ANTIBIOTICS

A reaction to antibiotics that either the mother, if breastfeeding, or baby is taking can cause diarrhea, nausea, and stomach pain.

PARASITES

A less common cause of diarrhea is intestinal parasites.

WHAT TO DO FOR DIARRHEA

HYDRATE

Babies with diarrhea are at risk of dehydration and should be hydrated frequently by feeding the baby breast milk or formula. Breast milk is especially good for baby as it hydrates and has natural antibodies to fight viruses. Your doctor might also recommend giving a rehydration solution like Pedialyte.

SERVE HEALTHY FOODS

If your baby is eating solids, be sure it's a healthy diet. Feed lean meats, such as chicken, and switch to bland, starchy foods like strained bananas, applesauce, rice, cereal, oatmeal, whole-wheat breads, or crackers. Probiotics in yogurt or in oral drops can help replace the healthy bacteria that your baby might have lost.

PRESCRIPTION

Depending on the cause, your pediatrician might prescribe an antibiotic or an anti-parasitic drug.

DIAPER RASH OINTMENT

Diarrhea is very acidic and can irritate baby's skin and cause diaper rash. It's important to change diapers often and apply diaper rash ointment to prevent diaper rash.

WHEN TO CALL THE DOCTOR

- Newborn baby

- Stool that looks like currant jelly

- Mucus or bad odor of diarrhea

- Bloody or black stool

- Severe diarrhea while taking antibiotics

- Fever above 100.4°F in babies three months or younger

- Fever above 102°F in babies 3–12 months

- Sunken soft spot on top of baby's head

- Sluggishness, drowsy, unresponsive baby

- Sunken eyes or cheeks

- Vomiting

- No tears when crying

The information provided is not a substitute for professional medical advice, diagnosis, or treatment. Always consult your pediatrician or health-care provider to ensure that a treatment is right for you and your child.

SNOTTY NOSE
BOOGERS YUCK

Stuffed-up noses come with babies getting colds. When that happens, babies can have a hard time breathing and eating. Because your baby can't blow his own nose, you are going to have to help. I could change dirty diapers any day, but cleaning out a snotty nose makes me gag every time.

TIPS TO HELP EASE A STUFFY NOSE

SUCK IT OUT

One way to help ease your baby's congestion is using saline nasal drops or aerosol mist with a nasal aspirator. While baby is lying on his back, squirt two to three drops into each nostril to loosen the snot, and then use a bulb syringe or nasal aspirator to suck out any mucus. Another option is replacing the saline with breast milk. Put two to three drops in the baby's nose to loosen mucus, and then remove the snot in the same manner.

VAPORIZER OR HUMIDIFER

Having a cool-mist vaporizer or humidifier in baby's room can help your baby breathe easier by adding moisture to the air. Be sure to keep the machine clean to prevent the growth of mold inside it. Use distilled water, not tap water.

LOVE PATS

By using gentle pats on baby's back while holding baby upright, you can help loosen and ease chest congestion.

WAIT IT OUT

Nasal congestion is a common part of babies having a cold. Many times, these colds will resolve themselves in time. If your baby is having trouble breathing or eating, or has a fever, you should consult your doctor.

NO MEDICATIONS OR VAPOR RUB

Traditional over-the-counter cold medications are not safe for babies. Vapor rubs (containing menthol, eucalyptus, or camphor) should not be used for infants.

NOTE: See your doctor if your baby is younger than two months old and has a fever or the congestion is making nursing or breathing difficult.

The information provided is not a substitute for professional medical advice, diagnosis, or treatment. Always consult your pediatrician or health-care provider to ensure that a treatment is right for you and your child.

FLAT HEAD
LEVEL-HEADED ADVICE

WHAT IS IT?

Flat head syndrome, or plagiocephaly, is a condition where a flat spot develops on the back or side of a baby's head. Because babies' heads are soft, and because babies spend so much time on their backs, especially while sleeping, pressure consistently occurs in the same spot, which can cause the baby's head to flatten on one side. This condition will improve as baby spends less time on his back.

2 TYPES OF FLAT HEAD

POSITIONAL PLAGIOCEPHALY

Called deformational plagiocephaly, it is the most common form of flat head syndrome, affecting half of all babies.

CONGENITAL PLAGIOCEPHALY (CRANIOSYNOSTOSIS)

This is a rare birth defect in which the plates on a baby's skull prematurely close. This results in an abnormally shaped head.

CAUSES (Positional Plagiocephaly)

- A baby's sleeping position is a common cause.
- Premature babies are more likely to develop this condition.
- A baby from a multiple birth is more likely to develop this condition due to his position in the womb.

SIGNS

- Flat spot on the side or back of the head
- Misaligned ears
- Bald spot on one area of the head
- Bony ridges on the skull
- Lack of a soft spot on the head

TREATMENT & PREVENTION

VARY SLEEPING POSITION

Switching baby's sleeping position can help reduce flat head. For example, if you put your baby down with her head toward the left, next time place your baby with her head facing to the right. You may need to gently turn baby's head to face the opposite direction.

EXERCISES

One of the most effective things you can do every day is baby exercises or exercises directed by your doctor. These exercises strengthen baby so she can sleep on her stomach safely. This stops pressure being placed on the same spot on the back of baby's head.

HOLDING BABY MORE

This might be a bit exhausting for you but holding babies more during the day will limit the amount of time they spend lying on their backs, which helps ease pressure on the flat spot.

QUICK TIP

A tip for remembering which direction baby's head was facing when you last placed him down is to put a pacifier on the mattress in the direction baby head was facing last.

POSITIONING THERAPY

This is a type of physical therapy that teaches you how to reposition your baby to aid in developing a more normal skull shape.

MOLDING HELMET THERAPY

In more severe cases, a molded helmet may be recommended. This involves fitting baby with a special helmet that helps correct the shape of the skull.

SURGERY

Surgery is usually needed in most cases of **congenital plagiocephaly** when sutures have closed and pressure in the skull needs to be released.

The information provided is not a substitute for professional medical advice, diagnosis, or treatment. Always consult your pediatrician or health-care provider to ensure that a treatment is right for you and your child.

HAND, FOOT & MOUTH DISEASE

HOLY CRAP, WHAT IS THIS?

Hand, foot and mouth disease (HFMD) sounds so awful but it is a common infection that affects children.

WHAT IS IT?

It is a highly contagious viral infection that spreads easily. It is characterized by sores in and around the mouth and a rash on the hands and feet. Occasionally, these sores spread to the legs, buttocks, and groin. These look more like a small raised red rash than blisters.

It is commonly seen in babies and children younger than five years of age. There are several strains of the virus, so your child can get HFMD more than once.

TRANSMISSION

- Spreads from person to person by contact
- Contact with saliva, mucus, or poop
- Airborne respiratory droplets from coughs or sneezes

SYMPTOMS

- Little red rashes or blisters on baby's hands and feet, in the mouth, and around the buttocks or genitals. These sores do not itch.
- Fever
- Sore throat
- Discomfort and feeling unwell
- Painful blisters on tongue and in the mouth
- Lack of appetite due to blisters in the mouth

TREATMENT & PREVENTION

There is no cure or treatment for HFMD. The virus usually clears up on its own within a week to 10 days. Until then, soothe baby and help by treating discomfort.

PAIN MEDICATION

If baby is experiencing discomfort and fever, you may be directed to give children's ibuprofen or Tylenol—**always check with your doctor before giving any medication.**

LIQUIDS & COLD FOODS

If your baby is experiencing pain when eating, try offering more milk or purees. Popsicles made of fruit juice or yogurt may also help soothe a sore mouth and throat.

HYDRATE

Make sure baby stays hydrated with liquids, breast milk, or formula.

GOOD HYGIENE

Frequent handwashing with soap and water and keeping toys and surfaces disinfected are two of the best ways to protect from HFMD.

NOTE: Contact your pediatrician if you suspect your child might have contracted the disease.

The information provided is not a substitute for professional medical advice, diagnosis, or treatment. Always consult your pediatrician or health-care provider to ensure that a treatment is right for you and your child.

THE FLU
IT'S ONLY A MATTER OF TIME

Flu can be dangerous for babies, and there can be serious complications. It is recommended that babies six months and older get a flu shot every year.

QUICK TIP
You will not spread the flu to your baby in your breast milk. In fact, your milk will help protect baby due to the antibodies contained in it.

WHAT IS IT?

Flu is short for the influenza virus. The virus infects the nose, throat, and lungs and is very contagious. It can range from a mild illness to one that is severe, even life-threatening.

When young babies or toddlers are affected by the flu, it can be very dangerous, even deadly. Children under five years of age are at high risk for serious complications. If you suspect your baby may have contracted the flu, don't hesitate to contact your doctor.

TRANSMISSION

- Inhaling the virus from someone who has it and coughs or sneezes
- Touching anything that has the virus on it

SYMPTOMS

- Fever
- Chills and body shakes
- Cough
- Sore throat
- Runny or stuffy nose
- Fatigue, not feeling well
- Poor appetite
- Vomiting or diarrhea
- Body ache

For more flu information, visit CDC.gov/flu or call CDC at (800) CDC-INFO or (800) 232-4636.

The information provided is not a substitute for professional medical advice, diagnosis, or treatment. Always consult your pediatrician or health-care provider to ensure that a treatment is right for you and your child.

SERIOUS COMPLICATIONS

- Pneumonia
- Dehydration
- Encephalitis
- Sinus or ear infections
- Long-term health concerns (heart disease, asthma, or blood disorders)

WHAT TO DO

Call the doctor right away if your baby has any typical flu symptoms and to find out if the baby should be examined to prevent complications.

REST

Help your little one get plenty of rest and keep activities to a minimum.

FLUIDS

Offer lots of fluids to prevent dehydration from fever and loss of appetite. Breastfeed or bottle feed baby or give baby Pedialyte if your doctor recommends it. If baby is eating solids, try giving the baby soup or broth.

PAIN AND FEVER RELIEVERS

If your doctor recommends it, you can give acetaminophen or ibuprofen to reduce the fever and alleviate body aches (don't give ibuprofen to babies younger than six months old).

ANTIVIRAL MEDICATIONS

Your pediatrician will determine if an antiviral prescription is necessary for your baby or toddler. Antiviral medications may reduce the duration of the virus, make symptoms milder, and prevent complications. These medications work best when given during the first two days of illness.

GET VACCINATED

The Centers for Disease Control (CDC) and the American Academy of Pediatrics (AAP) recommend vaccinations for children six months or older, caregivers, and parents every year.

We all
need a little
support,
especially if
you are a
parent.

SUPPORT

Finding help when you need it

CHILDCARE
WHAT TO DO AND KNOW

The decision to start childcare is one of the most difficult and stressful for any parent. Here are some things to know and tips to help make the transition a bit less stressful.

QUICK TIP
STAFFING RATIO
The ideal staffing ratio for infants to 12 months is one staff member for every three to four infants.

WHAT IS CHILDCARE?

Childcare facilities come in two types:

1. GROUP CHILDCARE

These facilities are similar to traditional schools and are state licensed. Children in childcare vary in ages from infants to three years of age.

2. HOME CHILDCARE

These facilities are run out of the provider's home. Some home childcare providers are accredited and have state licenses but many are not.

TIPS FOR CHOOSING CHILDCARE

DO YOUR RESEARCH

Get recommendations from family, friends, other parents, your pediatrician, online, etc. Start looking early, as some places might have a waiting list.

CHECK THE GROUND GAME

Pay attention to the ratio of staff to children and how staff interacts with them. Caregivers should be down at the child's level, playing with or holding babies. Babies need lots and lots of love and care for them to thrive.

HYGIENE POLICY

Find out how often the toys, surfaces, and spaces are sanitized.

CHECK IT OUT

Visit the centers yourself to assess whether one meets your needs. Look for:

- Current license
- Warm, friendly, & happy staff
- Clean environment
- Childproofed

- Stimulating daily activities
- Lots of age-appropriate books
- Lots of age-appropriate toys
- Shared space

MATCHING PHILOSOPHIES

Find out if you share the childcare's parenting philosophy on:

- Discipline (Do the caregivers use time-outs, scoldings, etc.?)
- Television (Is the TV on all day or used sparingly, if at all?)
- Food policy or plan (What snacks or drinks are provided for older babies?)
- Napping (When are naps? How are fussy babies put to sleep?)
- Sick-child policy (What symptoms prevent a child from attending?)
- Flexible drop-off and pickup times?

TALK, TALK, TALK

Make sure you communicate comfortably with the caregiver. In the morning, you should tell the caregiver how your little one slept the night before, if your child is teething, and whether your child ate breakfast. At the end of the day, you'll want to know similar information, such as the number of diapers used, when your child napped, and if your child seemed happy overall.

TRUST YOUR FEELINGS

If something feels wrong, keep searching. If something just doesn't feel right about the situation, investigate other options.

ADDRESS CONFLICT ASAP

If a conflict occurs, address issues right away, rather than ignoring them. Treat the caregiver with respect, but don't be afraid to speak up.

CHANGE UP

If things don't work out, make a switch.

BABYSITTERS
FINDING A GOOD SITTER

It can be really tough finding a good sitter and being comfortable leaving your baby with one. Here are some insights and tips for finding one a bit easier.

TIPS FOR FINDING A SITTER

REFERRALS

One of the first places to start is by asking friends, family, and colleagues if they have babysitter recommendations. Word of mouth is almost always the best. Also, be sure to ask what they pay their babysitter.

LOCAL COMMUNITY

Many local organizations like churches and libraries might have recommendations.

ONLINE APPS

Use babysitting online resources.

NANNIES

If you have a nanny, she may be able to suggest a sitter, or if you happen to visit your local park, you may find nannies there who have ideas.

YOU FOUND A SITTER, NOW WHAT?

INTERVIEW

You might start by having a phone interview to see if you feel this person would be a good fit.

BACKGROUND CHECK

If you go through an app to find a sitter, it may provide background check capability. But if you find someone locally, you can use one of the online background check companies for a small fee. To conduct a background check, you need to confirm a babysitter's identity. Ask for the person's full name, social security number, and driver's license. If your babysitter is not a US citizen, ask for her passport number and work permit.

MEET AND GREET

Meet with the candidate in person. Be prepared to ask questions regarding how the sitter would deal with issues like discipline. If the interview goes well, you should spend some time introducing the new sitter to baby. See how the sitter interacts with the baby.

AGREE ON THE RATE

It's best to agree on compensation up front. This will be determined by where you live, how many children you have, and how old they are. Local friends and family can help with this by sharing what they pay for sitters.

GET REFERENCES

Get at least two references who have used the potential sitter. Ask them about the candidate's experience and whether they would recommend the person. Inquire about the person's best attributes as well as weaknesses.

EXTRA THOUGHTS

Don't ask the babysitter to do other chores, for example, cleaning, doing the dishes, or laundry. You want the sitter to focus only on your child.

SET THE RULES

If you don't want anyone smoking in the house, inviting friends over, or texting and speaking with friends until the baby is in bed, you should establish these rules upfront.

Tell the sitter your guidelines for how much TV or what type of shows your baby is allowed to watch. Also, review what activities are allowed or not and where the sitter can go with the children, such as the park or other outdoor places.

Review what foods or snacks are allowed and whether there is a schedule you want followed, including when bath and bedtime are.

NANNIES
FINDING GOOD HELP

It can be really tough finding a good nanny and being comfortable leaving your baby with one. Here are some things to consider that will make finding a nanny simpler.

TIPS FOR FINDING A NANNY

FRIENDS & FAMILY

One of the great sources for finding a nanny is other friends and family. This should be one of the first places you look. Word of mouth can help you find a nanny who is looking for a new family.

AGENCIES

There are many agencies that specialize in finding and placing nannies. These organizations can be helpful because they take care of some of the vetting by performing background checks.

ONLINE SEARCHES

One way to find a nanny is to use one of the online nanny search engines.

OTHER NANNIES

Use the nanny network—nannies know nannies and they know who is looking. A good way to find a nanny is to tap into this network. How do you do that? First, speak to your friends and ask their nannies about anyone they may know.

Second, check out the local park—you will always find nannies and parents there. Speaking with them about potential candidates could provide possible recommendations.

COST

What nannies cost varies widely depending on where you live and how many hours the nanny works. The best way to get an idea of the going rate in your area is to ask other parents, and then ask each candidate for the person's salary range.

REFERENCES

Ask each candidate for a list of past and present references, and call them. They should provide a minimum of two references, although more is better. Ask those references specific questions: instead of asking whether they liked the nanny, ask what exactly they liked and didn't like about the person or their work, etc.

CONTRACT

Whatever your arrangement, you will want to put it in writing so that it is clear to everybody what expectations are. A written document can help outline the nanny's responsibilities.

Things to consider:

What hours will the nanny work?

How much are you paying?

What vacation time and holidays will the nanny have?

Are those holidays paid?

Are you paying an hourly rate or annual salary?

Will you provide any sick days?

Will you provide a gas allowance?

Do you want housework and cleaning done?

Do you want the nanny to cook for the baby and you?

Do you want the nanny to bathe and put baby to bed?

Do you have a schedule for the baby?

Will the nanny be driving the baby to the park?

Do you have specific baby activities?

Are playdates with other babies OK?

THE BIG INTERVIEW
QUESTIONS TO ASK YOUR NANNY

Having a set of question ready to ask candidates can be very helpful when you arrange a meeting with prospective nannies. Here is a set of questions to help you with the process.

QUESTIONS

GENERAL:

- How long have you been a nanny?
- How old were the other children you cared for?
- Do you have any formal childhood development or childcare training?
- Do you have emergency training? In CPR? First aid?
- If not, would you be willing to take CPR classes and first aid training?
- What would you do if my child was sick or had an accident?
- Would you mind if I ran a background check on you?
- Are you up to date on your Tdap vaccine (tetanus-diphtheria-pertussis/whooping cough) ?

BEING A NANNY:

- Why are you a nanny?
- Why are you looking for a new position?
- What do you like about the job?
- Describe your ideal family/employer.
- What do you like least about being a nanny?
- Do you have any problems with pets?

DEALING WITH CHILDREN:

- What are your beliefs about child rearing?
- What do children like best about you?
- How do you comfort children?
- How do you deal with separation anxiety?
- How do you discipline children?
- Give an example of a previous discipline problem and how you handled it.
- What are some rules you've followed in other households that you think worked well?
- Which rules haven't worked for you?
- Would you be willing to follow my rules and disciplining/comforting strategies even if they're different from yours?

LOGISTICS AND SALARY:

- Do you want a live-in arrangement?
- If not a live-in arrangement, where do you live and how will you get to work?
- If it's not a live-in arrangement, will you bring your own food or expect meals to be provided?
- Do you have a well-functioning car, with appropriate safety belts and room for car seats?
- Have you had any accidents, and is your car insurance current?
- Do you smoke?
- Are you willing to do light chores while our baby is sleeping? Which ones?
- Do you have any personal responsibilities or health issues that could interfere with a regular work schedule?
- When would you be able to start working?
- Would you ever be available to work evenings or weekends?
- Would you be available to travel with our family for weekends/vacations?
- When do you expect to take a vacation of your own?

Trying
to keep it
together one
day at a time,
ommmmmmm.

MANAGING STRESS
IT'S HARD WORK

The stress of parenthood will bring up many different emotions. This section talks honestly about those emotions and ways to help deal with them.

THE TRUTH
THE WHOLE TRUTH & NOTHING BUT THE TRUTH

When we were first expecting, I was told and not told many things. Some of those things would have been nice to know ahead of time, and some were complete lies. This is the honest truth that even your relatives and friends don't want to share for fear of being seen as the bad guy, insensitive, or inappropriate.

THE LIE: IT'S ALL SO WONDERFUL.

It's not all wonderful! Having a baby enter your life is a wondrous thing. You will experience many amazing moments. But there is also a lot of frustration, worry, and pain, and many aspects of having a new baby in your life are not what I would call wonderful.

THE LIE: YOU IMMEDIATELY BOND.

A girlfriend of mine shared that it did not happen right away for her, and I have to agree. I, too, found my babies beautiful and was happy to have them, but I didn't have some instant magical bond described by others. I will concede that a mother might have stronger feelings because she carries the baby for nine months, but I don't think it happens for everyone. I think bonds develop differently for each person, and loving bonds are something that build continuously over time.

THE LIE: BREASTFEEDING IS EASY.

It's different for everyone, but interestingly, many women told me that breastfeeding was not easy and did not come naturally. They shared countless experiences of not being able to produce milk or only being able to breastfeed for a short period of time. I heard some awful stories of things that went wrong.

So, if you are having problems, you are far from alone and should not feel any guilt! This was something many women shared with me too. They felt something was wrong with them or they were not good mothers if they didn't want to or couldn't breastfeed. **HARD STOP**. You should not feel bad at all. In most cases you already have to do the majority of the work, are tired, healing, and going through a hormonal tsunami, so if you can't deal with it or it's too painful to breastfeed, screw it.

THE LIE: WOMEN CAN HAVE SEX IN SIX WEEKS.

I read this and thought, Wow, I'm a gay man and didn't have all that stuff going on down below like new moms, and I was barely able to have sex at times. I was so tired; all I wanted to do was sleep. I checked in with lots of girlfriends, and here is what I learned: most did not feel the need to have sex right away.

They were tired, getting used to being a new mom, their hormones were a bit out of whack, and they were breastfeeding and body conscious. Some said they wanted sex because they felt hornier than normal; others had sex not so much for the act itself but for the loving validation that they felt desirable and beautiful to their partner. It seems like it depends on the person, but in my opinion, you should not feel guilty or rushed.

THE LIE: YOUR BABY'S SMILE MAKES IT ALL WORTH IT.

Yeah right. I love my kids so much, but when they are screaming bloody murder, I'm not thinking about smiles.

THE TRUTH: IT'S WORK.

Yes, it's work, and it's more work than you may think. Taking care of infants and toddlers can be exhausting and mind-numbing work. If you are taking care of the kids full-time, it's crushingly hard work. It is not a nine-to-five job that you clock out of at the end of the day to go home and relax.

You work from six or seven in the morning till around seven at night. Go to bed, get up, and do it again the next day and the next day and the next day and weekends too—this is rough stuff. And that's assuming your kids are sleeping through the night. For those who have childcare, I'm sure you consider it a blessing, but when you don't, like on weekends, even that is exhausting work.

Weekends used to be the time to catch up on sleep, run errands, and take care of chores, or do something fun for yourself. Be prepared: not so much anymore.

THE TRUTH
THE WHOLE TRUTH & NOTHING BUT THE TRUTH

THE TRUTH: IT'S EXPENSIVE.

Yes, yes, and yes. OMG, we have spent so much money on the kids; I'm amazed, and we are just getting started. I feel like I go to the store endlessly, and when I come back, everything seems to be for the kids. Diapers, formula, food, clothing, furniture . . . the costs mount up quickly.

THE TRUTH: YOU WILL BE TIRED.

People will tell you that, but I'm telling you, it's so much more. I have now experienced a level of exhaustion I have never felt before. Yes, I'm not kidding. If you ask new parents, they will all agree. The exhaustion is not just physical; it's mental exhaustion too. The combination is unbelievable.

My friends and family told me when I shared how I was feeling, that Yes, it's rough. They said in a year or two, it gets much better. Hopefully, you and your partner will work together to allow each other time to rest and find some "me" time.

THE TRUTH: YOU WILL SLEEP MUCH LESS.

Friends and family will tell you your sleep will be impacted by having kids. They are absolutely right, but it's a huge impact, especially if you are someone like me, who had a hard time sleeping before we had kids. Getting sleep is difficult. I always slept with one ear open, and now, with babies, my hearing has become supersonic.

I tend to hear every little movement and cry, even with babies sleeping down the hall. I have been told by many mothers that they experience the same thing. Maybe it's the mothering instinct. Ironically, my partner sleeps like a log and hears nothing, which many of my girlfriends tell me is just like their husbands. It must be something in couples: one person sleeps so lightly and the other is dead to the world.

THE TRUTH: YOU LIVE FOR THEM.

This is worth repeating. Your focus is no longer about your needs but all about them. It is very hard to ignore a screaming child or crying baby. You end up wanting to prevent your child from having a meltdown, so you learn to make sure your little darlings are fed, rested, and generally happy. You will be thinking and planning everything around the kids, as well as keeping a continuous eye on them to make sure they don't kill themselves.

THE TRUTH: YOU WILL FEEL SOME PRETTY INTENSE EMOTIONS.

One thing I found that no one will tell you beforehand is the intense emotions you may experience, good and bad, with your baby. I'm naturally an upbeat and happy person, but there is something about the whining and screaming of a baby that makes me nuts. One day, both my babies started whining and screaming. The combination really got to me. I felt an intense tightening in the center of my chest, and my body started stiffening. I was so incredibly angry.

I wanted them to stop so badly, I could have screamed. What also shocked me were the thoughts that were running through my head; the thoughts of physical violence I had were unbelievable. Of course, I wouldn't act on them, but they were there. I did not recognize this person; I had never met him before. I shared this with family and friends who were parents, and they admitted that Yes, they had also experienced some pretty intense emotions.

These feelings were so strong and intense, and it surprised me that no one had mentioned this was something I might experience. Also, I had felt so bad about having these feelings, thinking I must be some bad parent, only to find out this was a real thing. I can't imagine how birth mothers must feel: not only being tired but also healing and having their hormones working overtime. So, I'm here to tell you that you are not evil or bad because you have these feelings, and you are not alone in having them.

Some of the best advice my sister gave me was how she dealt with this: she put the baby down in the crib, or playpen, or some safe area, and walked away. Give yourself a minute to compose yourself, breathe, and find your center before returning to what you were doing.

POSTPARTUM

The birth of your baby is supposed to be one of the happiest times in your life, so why do you feel so miserable?

FORMS OF CHILDBIRTH DEPRESSION

There are three kinds of depression a new mother might experience after the birth of her baby. They may be caused by the rapid change in hormone levels that occur after birth.

1. POSTPARTUM BLUES OR BABY BLUES

A common, mild form of after-birth depression beginning within two to three days after delivery and lasting up to two weeks.

2. POSTPARTUM DEPRESSION

A more severe form of depression, it lasts more than two weeks. The symptoms last longer and are more severe.

3. POSTPARTUM PSYCHOSIS

This is a rare but serious condition.

BABY BLUES SYMPTOMS:

- Mood swings
- Anxiety
- Feeling sad or blue
- Irritability
- Feeling overwhelmed
- Crying
- Reduced concentration
- Appetite problems
- Sleeping issues

POSTPARTUM DEPRESSION SYMPTOMS:

- Insomnia
- Changes in appetite
- Intense irritabilty and anger
- Disinterest in bonding with baby
- Feeling sad and overwhelmed
- Withdrawing from friends and family
- Intense mood swings
- Crying a lot
- Panic attacks
- Thoughts of harming yourself or your baby
- Thoughts of death or suicide

POSTPARTUM PSYCHOSIS SYMPTOMS:

- Confusion and disorientation
- Obsessive thoughts about your baby
- Hallucinations and delusions
- Sleep disturbances
- Excessive energy and agitation
- Paranoia
- Attempts to harm yourself or your baby

WHAT TO KNOW & HOW TO TREAT:

THE BABY BLUES: Feeling sad and/or empty are very common and this usually goes away in two weeks. Rest when you can, and get help from friends and family.

POSTPARTUM DEPRESSION is a serious condition and needs to be treated. The common treatments for postpartum depression are:

Treatment: Working with a therapist, psychologist, or social worker to learn strategies to understand and manage depression.

Medication: An antidepressant medication may be prescribed.

POSTPARTUM PSYCHOSIS is a medical emergency. Call 911 and seek treatment immediately. Treatments during a psychotic episode include medications to reduce depression, stabilize moods, and reduce psychosis.

WHEN TO CALL THE DOCTOR

It's important to call your doctor as soon as possible if the signs and symptoms of depression have any of these features:

- Don't fade after two weeks
- Get worse
- Make it hard for you to care for your baby
- Make it hard to complete everyday tasks
- Include thoughts of harming yourself or your baby

WARNING:

If you have any thoughts of harming yourself or your baby, immediately seek help in taking care of your baby from your partner or loved ones, and

- Contact your primary care provider.
- Call a mental health professional.
- Call the National Suicide Prevention Lifeline at **(1-800-273-8255).**
- Reach out to a close friend or loved one.

I'M F*#KING LOSING MY SHIT

DEALING WITH STRESS & FRUSTRATION

Everyone deals with stress differently, but a crying baby who just won't stop pushes everyone's buttons. No one honestly tells you how frustrating and angry you might feel. It is completely NORMAL and you are not alone.

TIPS FOR DEALING WITH STRESS

SHARE RESPONSIBILITY

Whether you're a single parent or married, all the responsibilities of raising a baby alone are tremendously difficult. Caring for a newborn is physically and emotionally draining, and a lot for any single person to take on.

Make sure your other half is carrying their share of the work or you will quickly end up resenting them, a lot! If you are a single parent ask for help from family and friends.

TAKE TIME FOR YOURSELF

Taking care of a newborn is an around-the-clock job. For the first few days and possibly months, your newborn will wake up crying on a regular basis. This makes getting sleep really tough. Taking turns with your partner will definitely help take the edge off.

If you have someone who is responsible, trustworthy, and willing to care for your infant for only a few hours, don't hesitate to take them up on their offer.

There is a strange idea that you are not supposed to have a personal life once you have kids. Of course, things will definitely be different, but you can't completely stop your life. Do something nice for yourself-get your hair done, go to the spa-even going for lunch with a friend will make a big difference.

GET ON A SCHEDULE

The quicker you can get your baby on a feeding, sleeping, and play schedule, the more easier it will be able to regain some control over your time. You need to get on a baby schedule and track feeding amounts, sleep duration, even pooping and peeing.

Getting our kids on a schedule starting the second month was extremely helpful. The schedule helped us get the kids sleeping through the night when they reached 3-4 months of age. It was a lifesaver!

PREPARE BOTTLES AHEAD OF TIME

Preparing bottles the night before makes getting things ready for a hungry crying baby just so much simpler the next day.

SLEEP WHEN YOU CAN

Being on call 24 hours a day is grueling, and you will be getting only a couple of hours' sleep at a time. If you can sleep while the baby is down, it is great, but that is hard if you have other kids. Have your partner or the grandparents pitch in while you catch some zzz's.

Daddy Hack

Sometimes finding a moment to take care of yourself, from going to the bathroom, showering or doing chores can be challenging. You can always place your baby in a car seat carrier while doing these things. It's safe and you can see your baby and baby can see you.

I'M F*#KING LOSING MY SHIT
DEALING WITH STRESS & FRUSTRATION

GET PREPARED

There is an incredible amount of things to know when you are a first-time parent, and even the second time around. Getting prepared with knowledge and resources up front can help when the shit gets real. Many hospitals, churches, and midwifery organizations offer free classes to help you prepare. There are some incredible books on parenting, like this one, that help make the experience less stressful and easier.

GET OUT OF THE HOUSE

Having a stroller that works with newborns is very handy, as it gives you the ability to get out of the house to go for a walk or to the park. This goes a long way toward keeping you sane and relaxed.

JOIN A PARENTING GROUP

Sharing your experiences and feelings with others is a great way to get valuable information about caring for your infant.

IT GETS BETTER

As a new parent, your responsibilities are many and your stress level is high. Know that things do get better, especially as you get into a routine and baby is sleeping through the night.

AM I A SUPER-MOM?

This is the biggest bullshit I have ever heard. There is no such thing as a super-parent, and anyone who tells you differently is a liar. The habit of comparing how we are doing as parents to others is so unfair and unrealistic because every child is different, and so is every parent.

I did a tremendous amount of research putting this book together, and one thing I noticed that annoyed me considerably was the social-media parents who dolled themselves up and talked about changing diapers, dealing with sick babies, etc.

It's not real; don't get caught in this fake reality. Let's be real. Babies are hard work; it's exhausting, stressful, and messy. It's not a pretty Instagram moment much of the time. Don't even begin to believe that you are not good enough!

EAT HEALTHY

It can be hard for you to find time to eat, but it's important you fill up on things that are good for you. Drinking lots of water and eating healthy will help you maintain the energy you need to care for your newborn.

EMOTIONS WILL BE ALL OVER THE PLACE

You might go from adoring your baby and marveling at tiny fingers and toes to grieving your loss of independence and worrying about your ability to care for a newborn, all in the space of an hour. You and your partner will be tired and anxious, but stay patient and loving toward each other.

STOP GUILTING YOURSELF

Give yourself a break; if the laundry doesn't get done, dishes aren't washed, and you serve cereal or peanut butter sandwiches for dinner once in awhile when you're extremely exhausted, it's OK.

FINDING BALANCE
WHAT ABOUT ME?

TAKING CARE OF YOU

Starting a family is a lot of responsibility and a lot of work, but it's important that you don't neglect your needs in the process. Granted, you are going to be shifting your focus from yourself quite a bit, because kids come first. Even though this is the case, completely giving up any "me" time is not the answer.

You have to be able to recharge your battery at some point. If not, it will affect how you take care of your family, how you relate to your partner, and how you feel about yourself. There is no fix-all solution to finding balance, but there are some steps you can take to help achieve some level of balance.

TIPS ON FINDING BALANCE

PARENTING: IT'S A TEAM SPORT.

Working together as a team is extraordinarily important. Splitting up the workload so it becomes less overwhelming is necessary. Having one parent take over so the other can get out of the house to run errands, go to the gym, or get coffee is important. This has to be done so each person has an equal amount of downtime or out-of-the-house time.

If you are a working father and your partner is at home taking care of the kids, then when you get home, you have to pitch in. It might be the last thing you want to do, but your partner needs a break. For me, there are few things that are more exhausting than having to take care of kids nonstop, so step up, or you're going to create a lot of resentment that will ultimately affect your relationship.

GET HELP

If you don't have a partner to help out, consider a sitter or family members that can help, even if it's for only an hour or two. Even a short period of time out of the house, away from the kids, can make you feel better.

BE NICE

It can be really hard to be nice, considerate, and caring when you are exhausted, stressed, and frustrated. Believe me, my patience wears thin quickly, but as my partner reminds me, oh so lovingly, "Be nice." He is right: if both of you are loving and kind to each other, that will help you both deal with stress better.

Turn off the TV, put down the iPad or phone, and give a thoughtful back rub or loving hugs; these impromptu displays of affection make a difference.

PARK IT

Taking your baby to the park is a wonderful way to change things up. It's also a great way to meet other parents and nannies with kids. Having someone to talk with and share your experiences and concerns with can be very helpful.

PLAYDATES

Parents or nannies you meet at the park can be potential playdate opportunities. Spending time with other adults with babies can make you feel better and less alone.

SLEEP

Sleep is critical to being able to find balance. If you are tired and exhausted, when the baby goes down for a nap, you should too. Going to bed early will also help you feel better.

DATE NIGHT

Establish a date night for you and your partner. Hire a sitter and do something fun together.

GO FOR A STROLL

The fresh air is really good not only for baby but also for you. You can even go for a stroll at the local mall to get a change of scenery.

BIG THANKS
& ACKNOWLEDGMENTS

Where to begin . . .

I owe so much to so many for helping make ***Simplest Baby*** a reality. First, to all the parents out there, let me say how incredibly impressed I am with you. There are not enough thank yous to show gratitude for what you do. Now that I have my own kids to take care of, I have a far deeper understanding and appreciation for what it takes to raise and care for a family!

Parenting is hard, exhausting work and it's not a nine-to-five job. Taking care of the kids around the clock, you essentially are an on-call, all-day-and-night baby concierge: feeding the kids, dealing with a sick child, and the endless things that happen throughout the day. You just can't say, "Oh, I would rather not deal with this right now," and walk away. As a culture we really need to place more value on the care of children and those who do it—it is truly one of the most important things for our world.

To the donors and surrogates who helped us start our family, you are truly unique and incredible! Our family would not exist without the love and generosity of the gift that you have given us; our appreciation is beyond words.

Thanks to Paul and Tinti for believing in ***Simplest Baby*** and supporting and encouraging our vision. Thank you to Dr. Shaprio and Gabriella for sharing your expertise and knowledge with me and ultimately all the new parents who will read this book. Thanks to my editor for cleaning up all my work; as a person with dyslexia, I know it was a crazy hot mess. Thanks to Tressa and Lesly for all the support; thanks to my family and friends for sharing your experiences, stories, and just being you. Big thanks to our dear friends Chris and Oscar, and Harma and Asad, for supporting us and mentoring us on starting our own family; it meant so much to us.

Thank you,

THE SIMPLEST BABY PLAN
MONTH ONE LOG

SCHEDULES & LOGS

All schedules and logs can be found in the back of this book, or you can go to Simplestbaby.com to download the free Simplest Baby Plan forms.

SIMPLESTBABY LOG

DATE: _____

START TIME	END TIME	TOTAL SLEEP	TOTAL FEED TIME	FEEDING AMOUNT	BREAST STARTED WITH L | R	PEE	POOP	NOTES
					○ ○			
					○ ○			
					○ ○			
					○ ○			
					○ ○			
					○ ○			
					○ ○			
					○ ○			
					○ ○			
					○ ○			
					○ ○			
					○ ○			
					○ ○			
					○ ○			
TOTALS								

THE SIMPLEST BABY PLAN
3 WEEKS TO
3 MONTHS LOG

SCHEDULES & LOGS
All schedules and logs can be found in the back of this book, or you can go to Simplestbaby.com to download the free Simplest Baby Plan forms.

SIMPLESTBABY PLAN DATE: _____

3 Weeks to 3 Months – Day

TIME OF DAY	ACTIVITY		SLEEP	OZ FED		BREAST STARTED WITH		PEE	POOP	NOTES
				GOAL	ACTUAL	L	R			
7:00–7:30	Feeding	0:30				○	○			
7:30–8:00	Playtime	0:30								
8:00–10:00	1st Nap	2:00	AMOUNT SLEEP							
10:00–10:30	Feeding	0:30				○	○			
10:30–1:00	Playtime	0:30								
11:00–1:00	2nd Nap	2:00	AMOUNT SLEEP							
1:00–1:30	Feeding	0:30				○	○			
1:30–2:00	Playtime	0:30								
2:00–4:00	3rd Nap	2:00	AMOUNT SLEEP							
4:00–4:30	Feeding	0:30				○	○			
4:30–5:00	Playtime	0:30								
5:00–5:30	4th Nap	0:30	AMOUNT SLEEP							
5:30–6:00	Playtime	0:30								
6:00–6:15	Bath Time	0:15								
6:15–7:00	Feeding	0:45				○	○			
TOTALS:		HRS		OZ						

THE SIMPLEST BABY PLAN
3–6 MONTHS LOG

SCHEDULES & LOGS
All schedules and logs can be found in the back of this book, or you can go to Simplestbaby.com to download the free Simplest Baby Plan forms.

SIMPLEST BABY PLAN DATE: _____

3–6 Months – Day

TIME OF DAY	ACTIVITY		AMT SLEEP	OZ FED GOAL | ACTUAL		BREAST STARTED WITH L | R		PEE	POOP	NOTES
7:00–7:30	Feeding	0:30				○	○			
7:30–8:30	Playtime	1:00								
8:30–10:00	1st Nap	1:30	AMOUNT SLEEP							
10:00–11:00	Playtime	1:00								
11:00–11:30	Feeding	0:30				○	○			
11:30–12:00	Playtime	0:30								
12:00–2:00	2nd Nap	2:00	AMOUNT SLEEP							
2:00–3:00	Playtime	1:00								
3:00–3:30	Feeding	0:30				○	○			
3:30–4:00	Playtime	0:30								
4:00–4:45	3rd Nap	0:45	AMOUNT SLEEP							
4:45–6:30	Playtime	1:45								
6:30–6:45	Bath Time	0:30								
6:45–7:15	Feeding	0:15				○	○			
7:15	Bedtime	0:30								
TOTALS:			HRS	OZ						

THE SIMPLEST BABY PLAN
6–12 MONTHS LOG

SCHEDULES & LOGS
All schedules and logs can be found in the back of this book, or you can go to Simplestbaby.com to download the free Simplest Baby Plan forms.

SIMPLESTBABY PLAN   DATE: _____

6-12 Months - Day

TIME OF DAY	ACTIVITY		AMT SLEEP	OZ FED GOAL | ACTUAL		BREAST STARTED WITH L | R	PEE	POOP	NOTES
7:00-7:30	Feeding	0:30		Bottle		◯ ◯			
8:00	Playtime	1:00							
9:00-10:30	1st Nap	1:30	AMOUNT SLEEP						
10:30-11:00	Playtime	1:00							
11:00-11:30	Feeding	0:30		Bottle		◯ ◯			
11:30-12:00	Playtime	0:30							
12:00-12:30	Feeding	2:00		Solids		◯ ◯			
1:30-2:30	2nd Nap	1:00	AMOUNT SLEEP						
2:30-3:30	Playtime	0:30							
3:00-3:30	Feeding	0:30		Bottle		◯ ◯			
3:30-4:00	Playtime	0:45							
4:00-4:30	3rd Nap	1:45	AMOUNT SLEEP						
4:30-5:00	Playtime	0:30							
5:00-6:30	Feeding	0:15		Solids		◯ ◯			
6:30-6:45	Bath Time								
6:45-7:15	Feeding			Bottle		◯ ◯			
TOTALS:			HRS	OZ					

INDEX

SIMPLESTBABY

Join the Simplest Baby Revolution

The ultimate resource for the baby basics doesn't end with the book;
you will find more tips, more solutions, and more support for you at:

www.simplestbaby.com

Community

The Simplest Baby Community is a place to get advice and answers
to your parenting questions, receive encouragement, or share your own experiences
and knowledge with other new parents.

Blog

More tips, tricks, and advice that makes babies happy, parenting easier, and
moms and dads feel confident and relaxed

Free Downloads

Get the free essentials lists and helpful forms for:

Preparing For Baby Essentials List
The Essentials Infant Carry-on List
Packing the Perfect Diaper Bag
Baby Log Form
3-6 Week Schedule Form
3-6 Month Schedule Form
6-12 Month Schedule Form
and more...

COMING SOON
SIMPLESTTODDLER
AND
SIMPLESTPREGNANCY

Shop

Get the must-have recommendations for
products that make parents' lives easier while
saving them time and money.

FSC
www.fsc.org
MIX
Paper from
responsible sources
FSC® C012521